A Jew in Deed

Dr. Imrich Yitzhak Rosenberg, member of a delegation appointed by the Czechoslovak government to work together with the Soviet/Allied Command to deal with Jewish affairs in the territories first liberated from the Nazi occupation, August 21st, 1944.

Centre for Research
on Canadian-Russian Relations
at Carleton University

Slavic Research Group
at University of Ottawa

CANADA/RUSSIA SERIES

Volume 5

General Editors
J.L. Black
Andrew Donskov

CRCR

A JEW IN DEED

IMRICH YITZHAK
ROSENBERG

&

COREY
GOLDMAN

PENUMBRA PRESS

CRCR

LIBRARY AND ARCHIVES CANADA CATALOGUING IN PUBLICATION
Rosenberg, Imrich Yitzhak, 1913-1986.
  A Jew in deed / Imrich Yitzhak Rosenberg & Corey Goldman.
(Canada/Russia series ; 5)
Co-published by Centre for Research on Canadian-Russia Relations at
  Carleton University.
Includes bibliographical references.
ISBN 1-894131-60-6 (bound).--ISBN 1-894131-70-3 (pbk.)

  1. Rosenberg, Imrich Yitzhak, 1913-1986. 2. Jewish Anti-Fascist Committee. 3. Theresienstadt (Concentration camp) 4. Jewish orphans--Czechoslovakia. 5. Jews--Czechoslovakia--Biography. 6. Zionists--Czechoslovakia--Biography. 7. Czechoslovakia--Biography. I. Goldman, Corey II. Carleton University. Centre for Research on Canadian-Russian Relations III. Title. IV. Series.
DS135.R9R597 2004   943.703'092
C2004-905863-0

Canada   Canada Council
for the Arts
Conseil des Arts
du Canada

Penumbra Press gratefully acknowledges the Canada Council for the Arts and the Ontario Arts Council for supporting its publishing programme. The publisher further acknowledges the financial support of the Government of Canada through the Book Publishing Industry Development Program (BPIDP) for our publishing activities. We also acknowledge the Government of Ontario through the Ontario Media Development Corporation's Ontario Book Initiative.

TABLE OF CONTENTS

FOREWORD

Dr. Imrich Yitzhak Rosenberg called three quite different parts of the world home: Czechoslovakia, Israel and Canada. Born in Austria-Hungary, he grew up in the newly created Czechoslovakia, where as a young man he was active with the Zionist youth movement. As the following chronology demonstrates, the word "active" may be deceiving in that it does not convey the level of energy he devoted to his cause. Because Czechoslovakia was one of the very few countries to recognize its Jewish citizens officially as a nationality, he was able to campaign openly as part of a specifically Jewish political party. It is likely that this possibility provided Rosenberg with an unusual political consciousness, that is, an awareness of how the democratic process — no matter how flawed it became in Central Europe during the 1930s — had both an intrinsic value and could also be made to work to the advantage of everyone.

There is no need to repeat the history of Czechoslovakia and the disparate fate of its four official components, Bohemia, Moravia, Slovakia, and Ruthenia (five, if one includes the Sudetenland), during the 1930s and 1940s. Suffice to say for the purpose of this volume that Dr. Rosenberg was a busy participant in the growing Zionist movement and concomitant work, protecting Jews in Europe and in his own country particularly.

Rosenberg's fruitful labour on behalf of Jews during and shortly after the horrendous war in Europe is the subject of the essays contained in this book.

The story is told by Dr. Rosenberg, who in 1971 used both primary documentation and his own memory of the Soviet Jewish Anti-Fascist Committee, for a Political Science thesis. The tale is also told in part by Corey Goldman, a student of journalism, who made Rosenberg's achievement in connection with the transfer of 301 orphaned children, who remained in the Theresienstadt concentration camp after the war ended in 1945, the main subject of his thesis. Both research papers were written at Carleton University, Ottawa.

These are gripping accounts, yet they reflect only part of Dr. Rosenberg's life. They tell us nothing about his years in Israel and Canada, little of his personal life and his continued dedication to the protection and rehabilitation of the lives and heritage of Jews in Slovakia and elsewhere. The extent of his participation is revealed in the following chronology prepared by his wife, Dr. Truda Rosenberg. Two books related to these subjects have been published recently: Abraham Brumberg has edited a book of materials on the Jewish Anti-Fascist Committee and Susan Goldman-Rubin has prepared a booklet on the children of Terezin. Both are valuable and interesting, yet neither could begin to bear the personal association represented in Rosenberg's experiences.

As a closing remark, I dedicate my participation in this publishing enterprise to Dr. Truda Rosenberg, Imrich's long-time wife, defined in the best possible way: his love, his partner and his friend.

J.L. Black, Director
Centre for Research on Canadian-Russian Relations (CRCR)
Carleton University
Ottawa, Ontario
Canada

INTRODUCTION

DR. IMRICH YITZHAK ROSENBERG, A BIOGRAPHICAL SURVEY

Dr. Truda Rosenberg, 1987

1913

Born 27 May, in Nove Mesto nad Vahom in Slovakia. The Hebrew name for this city as it is found in Hebrew literature is IR CHADASHA. His father, who had been ordained as a Rabbi, taught Rabbis and also wrote poetry in Hebrew and Aramaic.

Imrich's lifelong devotion to Zionist causes began when he was fifteen, when he joined the local branch of the first Zionist movement called Hashomer — a Jewish boy scout movement established in the early twenties. This movement merged later with the Zionist youth movement called Maccabi Hatzair, which was a movement engaged in gymnastic and sport activities.

1919-1923

Attended elementary school in Nove Mesto nad Vahom and, from 1923-31, attended Stefanik High School in Nove Mesto nad Vahom. This was the only city in Czechoslovakia with a Jewish High School in the Austro-Hungarian Empire. During World War I, as the Austro-Hungarian Empire started to crumble, Czechoslovakia was established as an independent state and Czechs and Slovaks united to form a single country.

1929

As a high school student, Imrich remained active in Zionist activities. He was elected national chairman of El Al, a national Zionist high school students' association in Slovakia, which he founded. As chairman, he went to many cities with El Al branches, speaking to Jewish students and organizing youth groups. He also organized the first Zionist summer camps in Czechoslovakia.

1930s — At Tomas Masaryk's grave site,
in Scout uniform on the right.

In addition, Rosenberg served as editor of the weekly publication Hamaccabi, and was a regular contributor to the three weekly Jewish papers: *Zidovske Zpravy* (in Czech) from Prague; *Zidovske Noviny* (in Slovak) from Bratislava; and *Selbstwehr* (in German), a semi-official paper of the Zionist organization in Czechoslovakia.

1931
Elected to the Rosh Hanhala Arzit (National Executive) of Maccabi Hatzair, in charge of the Education Department. Maccabi Hatzair grew rapidly all across Czechoslovakia and became numerically the largest of all the Zionist youth movements. He was the ideologue and organizer of this movement, writing most of the leading articles in German and Slovak on the origins of Maccabi Hatzair.

Rosenberg became known as a dynamic speaker who was sought after by many other groups to debate with hostile Slovak journalists.

He debated in all the small towns in Slovakia, gaining the reputation of a fearless Jew. To earn a living, Rosenberg accepted the position of Secretary-General to the President of the Parliamentary Jewish Party in Slovakia (Zidovska Strana). From his income, he financed a large proportion of the secretariat expenses of Maccabi Hatzair. His duties included: preparing legislative work, speaking on political subjects during elections and acting as a liaison to other political parties.

Rosenberg travelled with Dr. Emil Margulies, then Chairman of the Jewish Party, to the larger cities in Slovakia, lecturing in Slovak on the importance of political awareness. The Party had been created to give Jews of Czechoslovakia political input in the Czech Parliament. In 1920, the Jews of Czechoslovakia had the right to their own representatives in parliamentary elections. From 1925 onward, the Jewish Party was a legitimate and recognized parliamentary political party representing the Jewish minority, and the Jews were part of every government coalition up to the infamous Munich Agreement in 1938, which ended the democratic system in Czechoslovakia. The Party played an important part in the mosaic of Czechoslovakia and was considered a constructive element in the defence of that country.

Continuing with his own growth in relation to Zionism, Rosenberg was deeply influenced by a number of Shlichim (Emissaries) from Kibbutz Degania Aleph in Israel, including its founders Joseph Baratz and Yehoshua Manoah. They helped shape his ideological perspective regarding the Zionist movement.

1932
Amidst his Zionist and political activities, Rosenberg began studying toward a Doctorate of Law degree, with emphasis on minorities and constitutional law at Komensky University in Bratislava.

1933-1935
Rosenberg visited Palestine for the first time, walking from Dan to Beer-Sheva. This visit left a deep impression on him. Upon returning to university, he accepted a position with the Jewish National Fund and assisted Dr. Oskar Neuman, the Jewish National Front (JNF) representative, as a public speaker in the Slovak language.

Rosenberg's articles in Czech, German and Slovak were reproduced in many Zionist weeklies across Central Europe. He joined the editorial board of *Zidovske Noviny,* the only official Jewish weekly of the Zionist organization in Slovakia. His subsequent editorials became the most cited materials in the Zionist educational process and are considered even today as essential to understanding the thirties in Central Europe. Rosenbergs' articles and letters have been used by scholars as source material for their Ph.D. theses at Israeli universities. Rosenberg was also responsible for the editorial end of all publications of Maccabi Hatzair.

In 1935, he became a member of the Hanhala Olamith (world executive) of Maccabi Hatzair, where he was responsible for the ideological development of this movement, which grew correspondingly in all of Western and Central Europe with the rise of the Nazis. He also played a significant part in its eventual merger with Gordonia, a pioneer (halutzic) movement strong in Eastern Europe and Palestine, just before the outbreak of World War II. The movement, resulting from this merger, became known in Eretz Israel as Chever Hakvutzot, and its most recent change within the kibbutz movement became known as Ichud Hakvutzot V'Kibbutzim.

1936

Continued his law studies at Komensky University, while pursuing his Zionist activities, and was elected to the Zionist executive organization in Slovakia.

1937

Appointed Secretary-General of the Maccabi Association for Czechoslovakia.

1938

During the stressful months prior to the Munich Agreement, 30 September 1938, Dr. Rosenberg played a part in the defence of his country, Czechoslovakia. He represented the Maccabi movement in the Czechoslovak Security Committee formed by the Sokol gymnastic movement at the request of the Ministry of Defence. In the May mobilization of the Czechoslovak army, he played an essential part in the creation and functioning of special semi-military units of volunteers formed from the membership of the Maccabi movement. These units played their part in those fateful months prior to the execution of the Munich Agreement by cooperating with the defence forces of Czechoslovakia. Generals Snejdarek and Milos Zak publicly expressed thanks to the Maccabi movement and its defence capabilities and publicly promised to fight along with the Maccabim for their country, Israel.

While the Republic of Czechoslovakia was in the process of disintegration, Rosenberg worked feverishly to establish and maintain reliable contacts between the two parts of the movement in Bohemia and in Slovakia, to achieve unity of purpose.

Many times Rosenberg was called upon by the highest defence groups, along with the head of the Sokol movement, to participate in the critical sessions of the defence establishment in Prague. At one such occasion, he stubbornly pitted the fighting spirit of the Maccabi group against the erosion and helplessness of the army leaders. During these fateful months, the Maccabi movement provided not only military support, but were the basis of the organized escape of Jews from Czechoslovakia to Poland, France and England.

When Dr. Rosenberg sought to keep the two Maccabi movements in Bohemia and Slovakia united, it was his intention to try and keep a solid framework of exchange of mutually valuable information on Bricha (illegal immigration to Palestine), and on the availability of visas for the countries of South America and the Caribbean Islands. Bricha activities included: purchasing certificates for Jews fleeing Nazi persecution and seeking refuge in Palestine. These efforts bore fruit when the necessity arose to flee Czechoslovakia.

In 1938, while involved with rescue work concerning Jews, Rosenberg visited Palestine for a second time and participated in the establishment of Kibbutz Kfar Hamaccabi.

During the entire period between 1933 to 1939, he was chairman of the Zionist University Students Association Ben Guria, at Komensky University. This group developed a large number of youth leaders who, under his leadership, were active in saving many Jewish lives in

1939 — Being introduced by his Rabbi, making a speech, Bratislava.

Czechoslovakia, Austria and Germany. At the time of the infamous
Kristallnacht, on 9 November 1938, in Germany and Austria, he participated in a small underground operation in Berlin that saved a number of Jews and moved them clandestinely over the mountainous border to safety in Czechoslovakia. Another organization located there
moved them overseas and to Palestine.

1939

In January, Rosenberg obtained his Doctorate from Komensky
University in Bratislava. Dr. Rosenberg then moved to the Hague,
Holland, to begin post-doctoral studies, specializing in minorities in
international law. He devoted most of his free time to Bricha.

The emigration and escape of Jews from Czechoslovakia started
immediately after the Munich Agreement and increased considerably
after the German occupation of Czechoslovakia, which occurred on 15
March 1939.

In this connection, Dr. Rosenberg travelled to London and established a Secretariat within the offices of the Maccabi World Union to

deal with Bricha. He then returned to Slovakia in co-operation with the Czech resistance movement in London, and helped direct the escape of a large number of Jews. He obtained an official document from the Slovak administration, permitting him to travel to any part of the country with a view of promoting "immigration" to Palestine.

He supervised, while in Holland, the contacts with members of the Maccabi movement in Denmark and England. Later Rosenberg was able to purchase about one hundred student certificates for university students in Bratislava for their immigration to Palestine. He collected money in Holland and England with the help of an introductory letter from Lord Melchett, then the President of the Maccabi World Union.

In the summer of 1939, he participated in a convention of Maccabi Hatzair in the kibbutz Kfar Hamaccabi. Upon his return, Rosenberg joined a delegation of Slovak Jews that negotiated with Msgr. Jozef Tiso, premier of the autonomous fascist Slovak government, to secure a relief for Slovak Jews. Anti-semitism was rampant in Slovakia. After the agreement between Nazi Germany and the Soviet Union was signed in August 1939, Rosenberg participated in the last prewar Zionist Congress held in Geneva.

The outbreak of World War II found him in London on a mission to deposit the money collected in Holland for rescue endeavors that included the chartering of Greek ships for the transfer of young Jews to Palestine.

He was appointed Honorary Secretary to Professor Selig Brodetsky, the Chairman of the Maccabi World Union and President of the British Board of Deputies. The Maccabi World Union was a liaison to the Jewish underground in fascist Slovakia, providing the basis for aid and rescue activities.

Dr. Rosenberg became a member of the Executive of the Merkaz Hechalutz b'Anglia, in which he represented the Maccabi Hatzair movement.

He also:

- Became Chairman of the Joint Committee of Czechoslovak Zionist Organizations in England. He founded the Czechoslovak

Maccabi Association, and was publisher and editor of the monthly publication *Hamaccabi*, which bound together all Maccabim, now dispersed to all corners of the globe.

- Broadcast regularly on BBC radio to Slovakia, encouraging resistance.
- Took over the Maccabi Self-Help Association, to which all Maccabim from Central and East European countries turned to for assistance and advice. At his initiative, all the various Jewish interest groups were represented as a unit. He also secured a valuable representation in the Czech Refugee Trust Fund. The co-ordinating committee of the Czech Refugee Trust Fund, developed during the war, was an efficient tool for saving and maintaining refugees. For his efforts, he received acknowledgement from Berl Locker, and Leo Herrman, the fund's first chairman. Professor Brodetsky and Edward Benes, President of the government-in-exile in London. Acknowledgement also came from the *Czechoslovak*, the official organ of the Czechoslovak resistance movement.
- Was appointed Chairman of the Bar Kochba, an organization of Maccabim from Central Europe.
- Together with Dr. Leo Zelmanovits, represented Czechoslovak groups in the British section of the World Jewish Congress.

They succeeded in founding the National Council of Jews from Czechoslovakia, which was in essence a continuation of the Jewish Party of Czechoslovakia, but in exile. He became its Vice-President and Secretary. The National Council of Jews, represented the political interests of the Jewish minority, vis-a-vis the Czech government-in-exile. The backing by Jewish soldiers in the independent Czechoslovak Brigade contributed to the Council's recognition as a successor to the Jewish Party of Czechoslovakia.

The first important consequence of the existence of the Council, was that at its suggestion, President Benes appointed Ernest Frischer, to the Czech State Council in London.

The second important outcome of the existence of the National Council of Jews was Dr. Rosenberg's appointment as the national

1941 — Merkas Hechalutz, London. Berl Locker is speaker.
Rosenberg is seated at far right.

Jewish representative in the Czech State Council's Name Committee.
He was assigned to the new administration of the free Republic of
Czechoslovakia, otherwise referred to as the Liberated Territories of
Czechoslovakia, in 1944.

In short, the National Council of Jews gave both Frischer and
Rosenberg an opportunity for political input within the Czech State
Council, as well as political involvement in the new administration of
the postwar Czech government. He was also on the Editorial Board of
the publication *Czechoslovak*. In addition, he worked closely with Jan
Masaryk, submitting briefs to him on the worsening situation of Czech
Jews under Nazis rule. This information was then related to the British
Government.

1940

Joined the First Czechoslovak Brigade in England, which in the early
stages was composed of Jews. They provided 90 percent of the men
and a small number of the officers. Dr. Rosenberg was active within
the Czech Army in speaking out on behalf of Jewish rights and equal

1942 New Year greeting postcard to Rosenberg who is in the Czech infantry training centre in England. The front of the postcard depicts pioneers in Israel working the earth.

The back of the postcard is on the facing page.

treatment within the Armed Forces. This Czech Brigade later became part of the Allied unit under the command of Canadian General Andrew George Latta McNaughton.

1941
Appointed to the information section of the Czechoslovak Ministry of Foreign Affairs.

1943
Appointed to the Legal Department in the Ministry of Agriculture and Public Works as Deputy Minister He drafted postwar legislation and edited publicity handouts for the exiled government of President Edward Benes.

1944-45
As the Jewish official for the delegation in charge of the new administration of the Liberated Territories of Czechoslovakia, Dr. Rosenberg was specifically appointed to represent Jewish interests in the delegation and to deal with all aspects of Jewish affairs in the Liberated Territories of Czechoslovakia.

Thus, on behalf of the Czech government and the World Jewish Congress, Rosenberg became the first Zionist to enter Moscow. He came from London via Cairo, Teheran and Stalingrad, to negotiate in a series of unique meetings with the Executive of the Soviet Jewish Anti-Fascist Committee, while the Red Army was approaching the Czech borders from the East.

19. VI. 1945.

List of children from Germany found in Terezín :

me :	First Name :	Birth date and place:	National:	Parents :
ugenreich	Dan	21.II.1942 Berlin	German	unknown
erlowitz	Asta	2.XII.1929 Elbing	,,	Father and mo-
erlowitz	Jakob	25.IV.1931 ,,	,,	ther without
erlowitz	Samuel	15.I.1934 ,,	,,	news.
erkmann	Günther	3.IX.1935 Koenigsberg	,,	Unknown –
ohnsheim	Viktor	29.VI.1941 Berlin	,,	Unknown
onradi	Irmgard	9.VI.1939 Dresden	,,	Dead
idelmann	Inge	31.III.1934 Frankfurt a.M.,,	,,	Dead
lsaeser	Käthe	25.VII.1933 Berlin	,,	Father dead,mo-
?aesser	Ursel	9.II.1931 Berlin	,,	ther deported b
lsaesser	Waltraut	9.IX.1929 Beuten	,,	Poland
elsenfeld	Disamel	2.VIII.1939 Berlin	,,	Deported to Pol.
anser	Carla	15.VII.1929 Hamburg	,,	Mother dead, father unknown
laser	Hanna	20. IX.1930 Berlin	,,	Mother dep.Pol. father unknown
lase	Jürgen	17. II.1936 Berlin	,,	Father in Belgim mother dead
eymann	Bela	5. II.1941 Berlin	,,	unknown
amaryth	Ruth	25. II.1938 Vienna	Stateless	
ahringer	Bela	10.III.1940 Bresslau	German	father in prison mother dep.Pol.
azarus	Berl	21.V. 1942 Berlin	,,	unknown
aier	Arthur	10.IV.1930 Karlsbad	Stateless	Father dead,mo- ther uninterest.
aier	Otto	15.I. 1932 Karlsbad	,,	dtto dtto
eyer	Tana	8.V. 1940 Delmenhost	German	Unknown,
eierstein	Hans	28.II.1936 Bresslau	,,	,,
eierowitz	Hanne	21.VI.1940 Berlin	,,	,,
uench	Benny	2. I.1940 Koeln		,,
uench	Tanah	23.IX.1939 Berlin	Stateless	,,
eumann	Hans	5.VIII.1929 Berlin	German	dead
ann	Krista	25.II.1942 Bremen	,,	Unknown
ann	Waltraut	27. I.1940 Bremen	,,	,,
afael	Margot	3.IX.1935 Berlin	,,	,,
osenthal	Jirka	17.VIII.1942 Berlin		
ovelsky	Gittel	23. IV.1942 Berlin	Stateless	dep.Poland
elbiger	Dan	15.VIII.1941 Berlin		
iegel	Gerda	19.X. 1940 Frankfurth a.M.German	,,	unknown
chrader	Beda	11.XI.1941 Berlin	,,	
homas	Gerd	1.II.1938 Frankfurt a.M.	,,	Mother dead,fa- ther uninterest
robel	Peter	17.II.1935 Muenchen	German	unknown,

1945 — Partial list of children found in Terezin (page 1).

He negotiated with the Chairman of the Soviet Jewish Anti-Fascist Committee, actor Shlomo Mikhoels; its Secretary-General, journalist Shakno Epstein; and poet Itzik Fefer. These negotiations were pursued

Name :	First name :	Birth date and place :	National :	Parents :
Auerbach	Judith	20.IV. 1942. Vienna	Autria	Unknown
Berger	Josef	20.VI.1933 Vienna	,,	
Ceitfeld	Thomas	27. X.1939	,,	Father Palest. Mother unknown
Gruener	Sylvia	19.II.1939	,,	Mother deported to Pol.Father unknown.
Hahn	Herbert	2.VII.1931	,,	Divorced
Kriss	Walter	23.XII.1932	,,	Mother dead,father in Shanghai
Rosenbaum	Brigitte	15.XII.1933 Eisenstadt	,,	dead,
Singer	Judith	17. II.1940 Vienna	,,	Mother in Pol. Father unknown
Sonnenschein	Feige /Litzi/	28. V.1939 Vienna	,,	Dead-,
Spiegel	Jakob	8.XII.1941 Vienna	,,	Unknown,
Schwach	Kamilla	12. VI.1932 Vienna	,,	Dead,
Zahler	Chana-Mindel	12. IX.1940 Vienna,Stateless,Father dead,mother dep.to Pol.
Zahler	Elfriede	17. IX. 1935 Vienna, Austrian,Dead.

1945 — Partial list of children found in Terezin (page 2).

with the idea of securing the Committee's participation within the World Jewish Congress. He obtained agreement from the Soviets, who had initiated this Committee during the war, in order to mobilize world

1945 — January
Appointed deputy to
Minister Jan Becko
by President Eduard
Benes.

Jewish support for the Soviet war effort against Nazi Germany. These
negotiations were processed through the many Soviet channels of the
Party and the government.

During the negotiations, Epstein and Fefer made many inquiries
about Palestine, the Zionist efforts and a Jewish State. It was therefore
no surprise when one day, Itzik Fefer informed him that "the Soviets
will be the first to recognize a Jewish State in Palestine whenever it will

be established." In December 1944, Dr. Rosenberg telegraphed this information to Eliyahu Dobkin, who was his contact with the Jewish Agency in Jerusalem.

While in Moscow, he met with the Soviet-sponsored Jewish Committee comprised of Polish artists and intellectuals. It was there that he learned for the first time the full scope of the Holocaust.

Dr. Rosenberg sat in on many meetings of the Lublin Committee and had direct contact with West Ukrainian leaders, including Dr. N. Frauenglass.

In Moscow, he paid close attention, specifically to any reports about surviving Jews found near the Soviet front lines. He transmitted names, occupations and addresses of Polish and Ukrainian Jews to Dr. Leo Zelmanovits in London, Rabbi Stephen Wise in New York and Eliyahu Dobkin in Jerusalem, so that families could be contacted. Dr. Rosenberg was aware that this was an important service at that time to inform the West of the full extent of the Holocaust. In addition, he made it a point to be accessible to stranded Jews who were found in war-time Moscow. He advised Jewish survivors in Podkarpatska Rus to leave the country for the West. This was connected to the first attempt to assist Jewish survivors of various concentration camps, who had been freed by the Soviet Army when the war was still on. He was in charge of liberated concentration camps behind the Soviet fronts, specifically in the supervision of repatriates in Carpatho-Russia in his role of Jewish Member of the government delegation for the Liberated Territories of Czechoslovakia. He established assistance and rescue channels to Teheran, through the American Jewish Joint Distribution Committee (AJJDC), for Jewish survivors.

His rescue and rehabilitation activities took him from Moscow to Lwow (Lemberg), where he travelled in military trucks to every concentration camp liberated by the Soviet Army. One of his main tasks was to organize a reporting system in Moscow, Lwow and Hust, which provided reports on concentration camp survivors, their names and essential particulars to London, New York and Jerusalem. His daily reports were transmitted via the Jewish Telegraphic Agency to all parts of the world.

On arrival in Kosice, Czechoslovakia, at the end of January 1945, Dr. Rosenberg was appointed by President Benes, Deputy Head to

Minister Jan Becko. In this capacity, he was put in charge of the Department of Repatriation for Kosice, Hust, Bratislava and Prague. Specifically, it was the Department of Social Welfare to which he was Deputy Head of Repatriation.

He acted quickly in his new appointment by establishing offices of this Repatriation Department in every new border point with Poland. As the front moved to the West, offices were set up in Hungary, Austria and Germany.

He received and distributed over 50 million Czechoslovak crowns to the Jewish camp survivors. Approximately a thousand people a day passed through these border points on their way to their former homes. Jewish survivors of all nationalities received food, clothing, pocket money, identity documents and railway tickets. Rosenberg established reception and health care centres for former political prisoners, Allied prisoners of war, and former prisoners of forced labour camps.

One of Rosenberg's responsibilities was the conduct of negotiations with the Allied High Command and later the United Nations Relief and Rehabilitation Association (UNRRA) and the International Refugee Board in matters dealing with the absorption of political refugees, then in German prisons, concentration and labour camps in all parts of the former Nazi Reich. He arranged for the repatriation of national units of Dutch, French and Polish prisoners of war who were found in Czech territory. In the midst of helping survivors, he was the key liaison between the refugees, the American Jewish Joint Distribution Committee and the Repatriation Department. Dr. Rosenberg also managed to secure the Czech government's cooperation in the movement of special repatriation trains, from Prague to Marseille en route to Palestine.

Rosenberg established repatriation offices all over Slovakia, including Bratislava. He also organized committees for the rebuilding of Jewish communities in Slovakia and the re-establishment of synagogues. He organized assistance to Hungarian Jews just liberated in Budapest, and helped to organize the Jewish community in that city.

After the liberation of Prague, Rosenberg established an office in that city, dealing with repatriation for the whole country, on May 9, 1945.

Then, on 11 May, he went to the liberated Therezienstadt (Terezin) concentration camp to take over its administration from the Soviet Army.

When he arrived at Therezienstadt, he began the repatriation of 30,000 survivors. He negotiated with foreign governments concerning the repatriation of their nationals, and he arranged for the quickest transfer possible of the survivors to their former homes. The camp was under quarantine due to a typhus epidemic. Those who were able to leave, left in organized transport to Slovakia, Hungary, Austria, France, Holland, Belgium and Denmark, while the Danish Red Cross was on hand to assist.

In June, Dr. Rosenberg transferred 301 Jewish orphans from the camp in 17 RAF planes enroute to England. In later years, many of these orphans moved to Israel, Canada and the United States.

He also provided Czech papers to refugees from the Baltic countries, supported illegal aliya to Palestine, and assisted emissaries who came via Italy from Palestine to Czechoslovakia. And for those who received documentation from the Repatriation Department, he made it easier for them to attend to their tasks without bureaucratic obstacles.

Dr. Rosenberg was in charge of possibly the largest single international rescue operation, which included the transfer of about 180,000 Jews from Poland across Czechoslovakia to Palestine and the West, after the pogrom in Kielce, Poland in 1946.

Dr. Rosenberg still found time, while helping repatriates and concentration camp survivors, to serve as Chairman of the Palestine Committee in Prague; Chairman of the American Jewish Joint Distribution Committee for Czechoslovakia in Prague. He also organized the World Jewish Congress office in Prague, and sent reports to the World Jewish Congress rescue committee in London and the Jewish Agency in Jerusalem.

In September 1945, he became a member of the Cabinet of the State Secretary for Foreign Trade in Prague. He also conducted research for bilateral commercial treaties.

1946

Sent by Jan Masaryk, as an official of the Czech government to the United States on an invitation to participate in one of the first United

1948 — Postcard depicts Prague in 1948, the year
Rosenberg escaped Czechoslovakia.

Jewish Appeal campaigns across the United States. He spoke on the same
platform as Eleanor Roosevelt and her son, General Elliot Roosevelt,
General Donovan and Rabbi Stephen Wise. The Administration
Committee of the World Jewish Congress assembled to hear a detailed
report on his negotiations with the Soviet Jewish Anti-Fascist
Committee. During the presentation, he was interrupted by Dr. Wise,
who got up and said in Hebrew: "Chatati" (I sinned; I erred).

Dr. Wise was referring to the following: sometime in the second half
of December 1944, Dr. Rosenberg telegraphed Jan Masaryk on behalf
of the National Council of Jews, as was previously agreed with him, that
the Soviet Jewish Anti-Fascist Committee had not made a commitment
on its direct participation or affiliation with the World Jewish Congress.
There was, however, a proposition that the Soviets might agree to a fifty-
fifty formula of voting power in all the areas of the World Jewish
Congress. These demands reflected the then obsolete figure of five million Soviet Jews. The voting power was to include the Soviet Jewish

Anti-Fascist Committee and participation in the Executive of the World Jewish Congress. He was aware that such a proposition would not be acceptable to the World Jewish Congress, but felt it was a mistake not to respond. Dr. Rosenberg had telegraphed the Soviet offer to Rabbi Stephen Wise, who at the time was a member of the Administration Council of the World Jewish Congress in New York. But Rabbi Wise did not reply in time, therefore, a rare moment of Jewish unity at the peace process negotiations was missed.

After his return from the United States, Rosenberg was threatened with arrest by the Minister of the Interior for his frank speeches in the United States. Therefore, he took a leave of absence to visit Palestine on behalf of the Czechoslovak government to report on the settlement of former concentration camp inmates. On his return to Prague, he helped Haganah representatives obtain weapons and contacts, using his home as the base for this activity.

Dr. Rosenberg was also Vice-Chairman of the Zionist Labour Movement in Czechoslovakia.

In the fall of 1946, he resigned from his position in the government in protest against anti-semitic acts in Slovakia against the government takeover of Jewish treasures left behind by the German Army in its disorderly retreat. These treasures represented manuscripts, artifacts, paintings and objects of art from many Jewish museums and institutions in Nazi-occupied Europe.

He fought for the return of this collection to the heirs of the original owners or to an appropriate institution in Israel, where most of the Holocaust survivors lived. It was not until the last Canadian Jewish Congress in Toronto in 1986 that his striving in this regard was recognized.

Working tirelessly on the resolution pertaining to the "Precious Legacy," he was happy to see the Congress pass it unanimously.

His wife, Dr. Truda Rosenberg, quotes her husband as saying: "Should it be my last act for the Jewish cause, I wish this to be known. It is important for our people to know our history, and our scholars must have access to it in a free world. The treasures belong to the Jews and are not to be kept in Czechoslovakia. The free Czechoslovaks are ashamed of their country keeping stolen goods and profiting from their display."

1948

The Communist takeover in Czechoslovakia took place on 28 February 1948, compelling Rosenberg to escape from Prague in March of that year. In May, he was sentenced in absentia by a Communist court in Prague to life imprisonment for his Zionist and pro-American activities, referred to by the Communists as "Zionist conspiracy" activities.

Rosenberg escaped to Brussels from Prague the day after Jan Masaryk's death. His passport was signed by Jan Masaryk. He was saved from being kidnapped in Brussels and shipped back to Czechoslovakia in March, by an official of the Canadian Embassy in Brussels.

1949

Dr. Rosenberg arrived in Ottawa as a landed immigrant, sponsored by the Czech ambassador to Canada, Mr. F. Nemec, who was a close friend. Unable to find employment for some years, he managed to get work as a labourer in the market, a law clerk, a real estate agent, a dishwasher and a pastry shop clerk.

1949-1971

Rosenberg later taught for some years at St. Patrick's College, at the time part of the University of Ottawa. The subjects he taught included: Eastern Europe, Soviet institutions, introduction to Marxist philosophy and the history of labour and communist parties. In 1954, Dr. Rosenberg became a Canadian citizen. From 1964 to 1969, he established his own successful real estate brokerage firm, Imrose Realties, acting as president. In 1970, he returned to academic life at the age of 57 to study in the Institute of Soviet and East European Studies at Carleton University. A year later, he obtained a Master of Arts degree in Political Science, where his thesis dealt with Soviet nationality policy during the Second World War and his own negotiations with Soviet authorities on Soviet Jewry's participation in the World Jewish Congress.

Rosenberg was Chairman of the Association of Czechoslovaks in Canada, Ottawa Branch. In addition, he was founder, along with Dr. Howard Trueman and Dr. Gibson (formerly of the Foreign Service in Ottawa and later President of Brock University), of the International

1984 — Rosenberg (right) talking with the famous Ota Hora.

Friendship House in Ottawa, which was sponsored by the Department of Foreign Affairs.

In 1971, Dr. Rosenberg and his wife, Truda, went to Israel, where he worked for the absorption of Jewish scientists in Israel, within the office of the Israeli Prime Minister in Jerusalem.

Dr. Truda Rosenberg, who holds a Ph.D. in Psychology, also worked in Israel. She taught in the Department of Education and Psychology at Haifa University, and in Oranim. She also directed the Psychology Department, which she established at Kibbutz Ein Harod. She was, in addition, the chief clinical psychologist for a large mental health centre and psychiatric hospital in Tirat Hacarmel.

1980

Returned to Ottawa. Dr. Rosenberg was invited by the federal government of Canada to serve as a private member of the Refugee Status Advisory Committee, which deals with demands for political asylum.

1985 — Imre and Truda Rosenberg.

He was a member of this Committee through 1984, and was also Vice-
President of the Czechoslovak Association for Arts and Sciences, in
Ottawa.

1981

Rosenberg had a lifelong passion for painting. Using mainly water-
colours as his medium, he painted a variety of subjects, including land-
scapes, flowers, old buildings, city streets, sunrises and sunsets. Among
many, he had a one-man exhibition in January 1981, at the National
Library and Public Archives, in Ottawa.

1986

Soon after Dr. Rosenberg's death on June 26, 1986, this letter appeared
in the *Canadian Jewish News*:

"With sadness, I read the obituary on the passing of Dr. Imrich
Yitzhak Rosenberg of Ottawa. It must have brought a tear to many an

1986 — Imrich
Rosenberg
(two weeks
before he died).

eye of the people whose path ever crossed with Dr. Rosenberg. The life
story of this remarkable man is how a community leader rose up to challenge the darkest days of the Munich betrayal, the collapse and occupation of Czechoslovakia, and the horrors of the approaching war. His
unlimited service to the Jewish community, his devotion to saving
Jewish lives, his efforts during the war and on the ashes of his liberated
homeland, stand as a living memorial for all of us ... to learn, to admire
and to cherish. To the list of his accomplishments may I also add that he
was instrumental in the transfer to England of 301 children, orphans,
from the Terezin camp during the Second World War. Some of these
children of Terezin live in Canada and share this loss with the 'family'."

PART I

IMRICH ROSENBERG

THE JEWISH ANTI-FASCIST COMMITTEE WITHIN THE CONTEXT OF SOVIET GOVERNMENT POLICIES AFFECTING THE JEWISH NATIONALITY

INTRODUCTION

To say that Soviet Jews have nothing in common, or anything to do, with Jews elsewhere is to run counter to the facts of life. To insist that the Jews in the Soviet Union today have no desire to maintain their national identity, or lack an interest in their own culture, is certainly for most Jews there, a negation of Soviet realities.[1]

This study arose from personal involvement in one of the rare periods of Soviet Jewish relations when the interests of the state and its Jewish people were seen as complementary. In most other periods, the policies of the respective governments, whether Tsarist or Bolshevik, were hostile to Jews and opposed to the preservation of their national identity. The Tsarist period was dominated by a crude and often violent policy of persecution, as expressed in pogroms and large-scale emigration. The doctrinal under-pinnings of Lenin's and Stalin's regimes were too inimical to a Jewish national culture and denied the existence of a Jewish historic people, as an entity throughout the world. Therefore, the period covered by this study from the 1880s to 1948, is reflected in a continuity of government policies against the Jewish people.

This study is concerned primarily with problems affecting the Soviet Jewry as a nationality. Lenin and his associates believed that the problem of the Jews was directly related to the social and economic system of capitalism. Therefore, once the system disappeared, Jews would disappear as a recognizable entity as well. Upon obtaining power, Lenin revised his previous policy towards Jews as a national group, recognizing them as a separate nationality. From this time onwards, the Soviet nationalities policy forms the framework for the understanding of the status of Jews within the Soviet Union. The present study analyzes in detail the successive periods of that policy, as reflected in the decrees of the Communist Party of the Soviet Union (C.P.S.U.), the policies of the government and the statements of Communist leaders.

Given this general sweep of political history, this study is also concerned with examining the origin, function and structure of the Jewish

Anti-Fascist Committee and its aborted role in reuniting Soviet Jewry with organized World Jewry. These developments occurred at the very same period when the Soviet government had created the Jewish Anti-Fascist Committee (J.A.C.) for other purposes than furthering Jewish culture and identity.

This study also traces the development of the J.A.C. from a state instrument for dissemination of propaganda to a cultural centre for Soviet Jewry.

For a better understanding of the growth and wide influence of the J.A.C. from April 1942 to 1947 (the Marshall Plan meeting in Paris), an analysis of internal changes within the Committee is related to the response of foreign Jewish communities and organizations to the many appeals from Moscow. A fundamental change in the outlook of Committee members was noted as a result of contact with foreign Jewish bodies, and in projecting the immediate and postwar needs of Soviet Jewry. The report on the results of an official mission of the J.A.C. abroad was in favour of the re-entry of Soviet Jewry into the mainstream of Jewish life.

A gradual change from confidence and cooperation to mutual distrust among the allies and the Soviet Union, in 1947, led to the Soviet Union's anti-Western political and ideological trend. Internal causes were also considered. These included an appraisal of the influence of a speech made by A.A. Zhdanov in August 1946, and a subsequent decision taken by the Central Committee of the C.P.S.U. in regard to certain changes in Soviet literature.

Consistent with this change in attitude was the suppression of the activities of the J.A.C. in the fall of 1948, and the arrest and subsequent execution of nearly all of its active members.

Included in chapters six and seven, are the result of research in the Library of Congress in Washington, the Archives of the World Jewish Congress in New York, the Library of the Hebrew University in Jerusalem, and the Central Zionist Archives in Jerusalem.

CHAPTER I

The emergence of the Jewish problem in Russia in the 1880s, from a backwater of Tsarist interest to the foremost place on the agenda of the government, was caused by a number of factors. Among the more important ones were: first, the nearly complete isolation of Russian Jews in the Pale of Settlement; second, their incredible poverty caused and maintained by the restrictive policies of successive Tsarist governments; third, their lack of full equality with the Russian subjects of the Tsar, which served to verify their already second-class status. The Jews were, in addition, suspected of being the ringleaders of the revolutionary activities performed by a certain section of the Russian intelligentsia, particularly after it became known that individual Jews in fact participated in the clandestine terroristic activities of such groups as Narodnaya Volya. Therefore, shortly after the accession of the reactionary Alexander III, a decision was made to create a special Imperial Commission to "investigate the Jewish question in Russia."[2]

The commission concluded its work with recommendations favorable to the Jews. One of the members of the commission, Demidov, even "advocated the abolition of the Pale and the granting of equal rights to the Jews."[3] The recommendations were, however, not acceptable to the Tsar or to his influential advisor and former tutor Pobedonostsev. Notwithstanding the public demonstrations of sympathy in New York and London, and the official condemnation of anti-Jewish measures by Gladstone, Pobedonostsev remained in his position of influence, and his policies were continued. Pobedonostsev re-established absolutism and Greek Orthodoxy as the two dominant supports of the empire. It came as no surprise that the despotic measures enforced with the approval of the Tsar soon after the declaration of these principles affected not only the Jews, but all rival religions such as the Catholics, Lutherans and

Armenians. Pobedonostsev was more specific in dealing with the Jews as a comment reputedly stated by him indicates:

> "... one third of the Jews in Russia would be forced to emigrate, another third would be compelled to accept baptism, and the remainder would be brought to the verge of starvation."[4]

Except for a small number of converts, mostly among the more prosperous professional Jews who lived outside the Pale, the other two aspects of Pobedonostsev's policy, namely, starvation and forced emigration, were successfully pursued by the government. These measures substantially contributed to an inner revolution among the Russian Jews, who in the next decade lived through one of the most important periods of their long history.

For nearly a hundred years, since 1791, Jews were forced to live in a particular area of the empire, the Pale of Settlement. Physical mobility was restricted outside the Pale, and Jews were further subjected to no less than 600 discriminatory legal enactments, half of them passed in the second quarter of the nineteenth century. Most of these laws were drafted "almost entirely under the immediate supervision of the Tsar."[5]

What reasons were given for the establishment of the Pale of Settlements? Rosenthal reports that the official motive behind the establishment of the Pale was "the protection of the less enlightened Russian people, against the economic enslavement ... by the Jews."[6] However, the real reason is stated to have been a fear of "the religious influence of the Jews over the Russians."[7] The history of this fear dates back to the end of the fifteenth century, when the spread of Judaizing ideas was considered by the then Russian elite as a danger to the integrity and future unity of the state.

It is hardly surprising that the long period of oppressive anti-Jewish legislation would have some unifying effect on Russian Jewry. Segregated in the Pale by the Tsarist government, and subjected to a variety of discriminatory measures which singled them out as people, the Jews were viewed as a close-knit homogeneous community, with a common interest and political destiny. The Russian Jewry was, however, not a homogeneous group, but a highly fragmented one. It is therefore important for the understanding and evaluation of the great changes, which occurred within Russian Jewry between 1890-1906, that the divisions among them be analyzed. Levin, a leading member of Russian Jewry and deputy in the first Duma, wrote:

"I doubt whether there was anywhere another Jewish group as heterogeneous and as motley as was Russian Jewry before it was physically destroyed by the great revolution."[8]

In the 1890s Russian Jewry consisted of three main distinctive groups: the Polish Jews, northwestern or Lithuanian Jews and southern Jews. The latter coming principally from the areas of New Russia, the Ukraine, Bessarabia, and the Crimea. Each of these groups was known by its distinctive character, shaped by the human and geographical environment in which it lived. There was nearly as much difference between the Lithuanian and southern Jew, as there was between the peasants of the two areas. The Lithuanian Jew was characterized as a pure intellectualist, represented by the formalist orthodoxy of the Gaon of Vilna; the Ukrainian Jew, on the other hand, was typified as an optimist who loved life and lived it to its fullest. For example, a Ukrainian Jew who produced the great Baal Shem Tov, was the founder of Chasidism. There was an even greater difference between the two groups and Polish Jewry. Poland was a conquered country and remained foreign. "The same foreignness," wrote Levin, "was felt by the Russian Jew among the Polish Jews. Even their pronunciation of Yiddish words were so different that often they had difficulty in understanding each other."[9]

The fragmentation of Russian Jewry was one of the results of the changing Tsarist policies, and posed a fearful task to any emerging national leadership. In addition, there were serious divisions on the political horizon. The last decade of the nineteenth century witnessed the formation of two opposing political movements, which represented the two major organized approaches to the Jewish question in Russia. In 1897, the Bund, a Jewish social democratic organization, was founded in Vilna. In the same year, a strong Jewish delegation from Russia participated in the first Zionist Congress in Basel, Switzerland.

Both movements left a lasting mark within the political body of world Jewry.[10] Both movements were under constant attack from militant Jewish orthodoxy, otherwise known as Pillars of the Law. The great mass of the Jewish population remained outside any movement, preferring emigration as the solution to their problems.

On the campuses of the universities of Berlin, Bern and Geneva, Jewish students who were prevented from attending universities in Russia formed Russian-Jewish scientific societies. These societies provided excellent debating forums for the two main divisions in modern Jewish thought, which included the Zionists on one hand and the Bundists on the other. Personalities such as Parvus, Helphand, Plekhanov, the economist Baranovsky, and the brilliant Marxist theoretician Struve, who later became one of the right-wing leaders of the Kadets, participated in the debates. One debate, between Plekhanov and Weizman, later the first President of Israel, became well known for its historical importance. In a letter to a co-worker, Weizman described the atmosphere and the issues:

> "... Davidson (a former Bundist) thought that there was the opportunity to finish off Zionism and Zionists then and there. They reckoned that Plekhanov would have the last word, but nothing of the sort happened. Mr. Plekhanov was debunked and routed, and retreated in the most ignominious manner ... This has never happened in Switzerland before. Just think of it: Plekhanov, the favorite, the idol who is worshipped so, and Davidson, who had betrayed the Bund as well, groveling before him." [11]

Most of the Jewish students returned to Russia after completing their studies abroad. These students became the leading intellectual elite within the Jewish communities, and later some of them were among the first elected leaders to represent the Jewish population in Russia. But several years were to elapse before these democratic trends could become a reality. One Jewish institution, which partly impeded this progress, was the shtadlan: a non-elected "backstair negotiator without a genuine status."[12] He used his community influence and money to obtain informal concessions for the Jews from the Tsar's corrupt officials. The Tsar's officials, on the other hand, fully recognized that the shtadlan was a good institution to affect stronger controls on Russian Jewry. However, the institution of the shtadlan soon began to lose its influence, when its numerous holders were ineffectual in stopping the pogroms. Jews increasingly began to organize themselves for self-defence, refusing to be left at the mercy of some mediating mendicant. The institution of the shtadlan was therefore cast aside in this process of internal revolution among the Jews, and new, more representative institutions began to rise to take its place. The Jewish Labor and national movements were both symbols of a new epoch "perhaps the greatest epoch of activity in all history of the Diaspora."[13] But as the internal revolution among Russian Jews continued to slowly transform the masses into a national group, the Tsarist government extended its policy of expelling Jews from some cities, and organized pogroms against them in others. The Kishinev pogrom of 1903 was the beginning of a series of pogroms, which exposed the utter helplessness of Jews, and the state of decay, despair and chaos within the government. The Minister of Interior Plehve considered the pogroms against the Jews as "a safety valve for the revolutionary restlessness of the Russian people."[14] But Levin saw in them "the ghastly rottenness, which had eaten into the system of the government," and "the beginning of the final collapse of the Russian imperial government."[15] Soon after the pogrom in Kishinev, came the war with Japan. Apparently unconnected, the two were manifestations of one destructive motif. The war against Japan was declared against the advice of the head of the cabinet (Count Witte), the foreign minister (Lamsdorf), and the war minister (Kuropatkin).[16] The Tsar heeded the advise of Plehve. When Witte reproached Plehve, the latter reputedly answered: "You don't know the conditions in Russia. We must have a successful little war in order to stave off revolution."[17] The war was lost. Instead of victory, the government was faced with serious political and economic problems. It avoided meeting them and generally continued to give the appearance "of an impregnable fortress, when in fact it was only a facade."[18]

In summary, it is possible to visualize this period as a continuation of the Pobedonostsev program, at times intensified through sudden violent expulsions and government-sponsored pogroms. Jews were made the scapegoat for every possible failure, and for everything wrong with the country, from a faulty economy to the wrong expedition of a war.

The reaction of Russian Jews to all these oppressive measures stiffened, but there was not, at least by 1905, a general consensus as to the response that should be adopted. To the politically more advanced among them, it was clear that the conditions for the Russian Jews would only change for the better, with a change in the regime. "But," commented Levin, "we did not think of that change in the form of a social revolution. We thought it sufficient if we could achieve a constitution like that, for instance, of England or France."[19]

The two Jewish political movements, the nationalists and socialists changed their programs in the last eight years of this period, and progressed toward a more realistic approach to the Jewish question. This realistic approach took the form of attempts by the Zionists to achieve Gegenwartsarbeit, that is, civic and cultural improvements for the Jews in Russia. The Socialists, on the other hand, as they attempted to gain popular support among the Jewish masses, advocated national cultural autonomy, along with their program of class struggle. For this doctrinal change, they earned the permanent and hostile criticism of Plekhanov and Lenin.[20]

These mutual adjustments also reflected on one feature of the original Zionist political program formulated largely by West European Jews; namely, the lack of Zionist interest in the separate struggles of various Jewish groups in their own countries. As a consequence, a large section of middle-class Jews withdrew from the struggle for emancipation. This was also the case in Russia. Only when the Zionists adopted the program of Gegenwartsarbeit as part of their strategy to "conquer the Jewish communities," did the Jewish middle-class in Russia join in the struggle for civic equality.

CHAPTER II

POLITICAL DEVELOPMENTS FROM 1905 TO 1917

The year 1905 was as important to Russian Jews as to other Russian subjects, aspiring for more freedom. Yet, there were significant differences. That year was "the most fearful year in the modern history of Russian Jewry,"[21] because of the appearance of the so-called Black Hundreds.[22] This organization, which was financially supported by the Tsar, was aimed at eradicating freedom as a whole, but "spent nine-tenths of its fury on the Jewish people."[23] It was a known secret that the official, central government, on numerous occasions, sponsored mob pogroms but it is really from this period that the Tsar himself became directly identified with the Black Hundreds. (See the admission of official sanction by Plehve to Dr. Herzl, the Zionist leader.[24]) The knowledge of this fact had a tremendous impact on the emerging Jewish national leadership, and contributed to the more bold approaches to Russian politics adopted by them. In effect, three distinct Jewish responses to the Tsarist policies can be distinguished during the revolutionary stirrings of 1905. The first response dealt with the right to submit petitions to the Tsar. The second response dealt with the invitation to submit suggestions as to how to improve the well-being of the state.[25] And the third response dealt with the elections to the first Duma. Nothing contributed more to the development of a general awakening to political life among Russian Jews and to a molding of a more unified organized national Jewish leadership, than these three decrees or manifestos.

The first reaction, in which whole Jewish communities participated, came in response to an imperial *ukaz* (decree), issued in December 1904, which promised Jews gradual improvements. The Jews were not satisfied with this pittance, and demanded implementation of civic, political and national rights. Thirty-one communities of the northwestern provinces participated in the petitioning of the Tsar, and twenty-six others from Moscow and Odessa. The tone of the Jewish demands can be detected from the draft of the petition submitted by the Vilna community:

"As a cultural nation, we demand the same rights of national-cultural self-determination which ought to be granted to all nationalities that go to make up the Russian body politic." [26]

All petitions were addressed to Sergei Witte, the President of the Committee of Ministers, who alone among the ministers maintained that there were justified reasons for the attitude which Jews took towards Tsarist authority.[27] He stated, for instance, that it was all due "to the sad material conditions in which the bulk of Jews live."[28] The petitions brought no changes in the status of Jews, either as individuals or as a national group, and all the onerous restrictions continued in force. However, in drafting and collecting these petitions, a new leadership emerged within the Jewish communities, consisting of educated men devoted to the ideals of civil rights and increased political freedoms for all Russian subjects. Most of these new leaders studied secular arts at foreign universities and were well acquainted with political trends and struggles abroad. Therefore, they now found common cause with other liberal Russians who similarly advocated more freedoms for all Russians. This "meeting of the minds" between the intellectual elite of Russian Jewry and other liberally minded Russians, helped to end the cultural and political isolation of Jews. On the Russian side, the liberal movement embraced such organizations as the Leagues of lawyers, engineers and railroad workers, and particularly included a number of outstanding legal experts who defended Jews accused of provoking pogroms. The ties established between Jews and Russians led to future political cooperation in the Duma. The Tsarist invitation to submit suggestions as to how to improve the well being of the state, brought an avalanche of resolutions, declarations and submissions. Most of them expressed demands for constitutional monarchy, similar to the one in England.[29]

The third manifesto, that of October 17, 1905, came in the midst of considerable industrial turmoil, when nearly all work in Russia was suspended, and the striking workers forced the factories to close down.

It was this manifesto that brought the promise of a new constitutional order and the hope for all, including the Jews, that they might achieve equality and freedom. Levin wrote of the general mood which followed the manifesto:

> "… We sometimes read of blind men who suddenly regain their sight. Something of what such a man feels when the light bursts open his brain was felt in Russia when that manifesto was published. Strangers embraced each other on the streets." [30]

This feeling of a new epoch was, as far as the Jews were concerned, mixed with agony and fear. While the Tsar's manifesto spoke of the "new order," another type of order was given to the Black Hundreds to fulfill. During the one week of October 18 to 25, 1905, "there were more than fifty bloody pogroms in various Jewish centres and several hundred 'bloodless' pogroms, involving plunder and property damage."[31] While Jews intensively participated in the election campaign for the first Duma,[32] they were also preoccupied with other vital matters. The need for better measures of self-defence was, of course, evident, but there was also the need to present a united political front at this crucial period. As chapter one has shown, this was by no means to be an easy task in such a heterogeneous community.

During 1905 a Russian national Jewish organization for the defence of Jewish rights operated for six full months in many parts of the country, and for the first time in the history of Jewish emancipation, a Jewish group emerged openly as a national political entity.[33] This organization was known as the League for the Attainment of Full Rights for the Jewish people of Russia. The refusal of the Bund and other Jewish socialist organizations to join the League because of the latter's "bourgeois" character did not detract much from the general support this organization received from the Jewish community. This fact, perhaps, gives some indication of the extent to which the Socialists had any political influence within the Jewish community during the 1905 revolution.

The League was founded at a constituent conference in Vilna, at the end of March 1905. The initiative came from St. Petersburg. The leaders were Maxim Vinaver,[34] the liberal G.B. Sliosberg; the lawyer Leonte Bramson; the Zionist Dr. Shmarya Levin; the historian S.M. Dubnov;[35] and the social revolutionary M. Ratner.[36] "The conferees," wrote Harcave, "agreed to form a league and not a party, because they hoped that the new body would speak for all Jews, irrespective of political association."[37] This was the first Jewish organization which made the important distinction between "national" and "civic" rights, and demanded the achievement of both for Russian Jews. "National rights," according to the published program of the League,[38] meant "freedom of national-cultural self-determination in every form, especially broad communal autonomy, freedom of language, and of education in the schools."[39]

The League considered the public platforms of the various political parties, but opted for the policies advocated by the Constitutional Democratic Party (the Kadets).[40] There was a consensus at the third convention of the League that, "despite the atmosphere of repression and the admitted short-comings of the Duma as a representative body,"[41] Jews will participate in the election. It was considered important that they should participate in order to have a voice in the Duma and to be able to assist the liberal and progressive elements in the attainment of equality for all Russian subjects. Jewish participation in the election served to emphasize the point, that for the first time the Jewish political elite joined forces with other like-minded Russians to endeavor to wrest away some measure of liberal democratic freedom from the Tsarist regime. Local election agreements were made with any party whose program supported the aims of the League, however, the Jews supported the Kadets. In other places, the Jews joined Polish and Ukrainian groups. Usually, the candidate of a nationality with the largest number of votes in a locality, got their support. Jewish election activities were intensive, and in the Pale the coalition of Jews and Kadets won many victories. In all, twelve Jewish deputies were elected, six of whom were Zionists.[42] It was proposed that the Jewish deputies organize a parliamentary faction, but this was opposed by the other six members, and a compromise was reached to consult among themselves on all matters affecting Jewish rights.[43] An interesting incident occurred when the Jewish deputies in the Duma registered their nationality and religion. It was expected that there would be twelve names repeated under the list of religions and nationalities. But, for instance, Dr. Gregory Yollos registered as Jew by religion and Russian by nationality, while his friend Solomon Gerzenstein registered as Russian Orthodox by religion and Jew by nationality.[44]

The election campaign, in itself, marked an important stage in the development of Jewish group participation in Russian national affairs, as distinct from the participation of individual (mostly former) Jews in Russian political parties. The election of twelve Jewish deputies represented the high water mark of Jewish political activities, even though the Jews should have secured twenty-three seats. The twelve deputies represented about six million Jews. They were the first formal political expression of the hopes and longings of the Jewish population, and they worked towards achieving necessary constitutional reforms and the establishment of a *modus vivendi* for the Jews within a more liberal Russia.[45] As history has shown, these efforts were in vain. While Jewish deputies and other Jewish political leaders worked for reforms and adjustments, the government with the support of the mobs continued the Pobedonostsev policies of oppression, pogroms and starvation. All these measures were ostensibly aimed at one solution to the Jewish problem in Russia; namely, their complete removal from Russian soil. Therefore, the floodgates were opened for a forced emigration of Jews to Western Europe, the United States and Palestine. Since 1906, a certain decline in political activities among Jews took place, which lasted until 1917.

With the rising influence of the Bundists, the Zionists and a number of smaller middle-class national parties, a new phenomenon appeared in the historical development of the Kehilah (or Kahal). It was the final separation of secular communal leadership from the all-encompassing leadership of the religious leaders, and it took place during the revolution of 1905. The traditional Jewish institution of the Kehilah, acted as a mediating influence between the Jews and the government. As with the *shtadlan*, the government devised ways to use the institution to effect controls over the Jewish population.[46] The Kehilah was given some responsibility to collect taxes, supervise elementary educational facilities and compile lists of potential military recruits of Jews for the Tsarist forces. This separation of the secular from the religious helped to foster plural political outlooks within the Jewish community. The only consequence was that various political parties were organized to reflect the main trends of political and social opinions. These were: The Zionist Party, which was the largest and best organized; the "Jewish People's Group," which was opposed to the Zionist concept and restricted its demands to civil emancipation; the "Jewish National Party," (*Folkspartay*) representing Dubnov's views on national autonomy;[47] and the "Jewish Democratic Group," with strong leanings to the political left. There were also four Jewish socialist parties: the Bund, General Jewish Worker's Brotherhood of Lithuania, Poland and Russia (in Yiddish *Der Algemeyner Idisher Arbeter Bund in Rusland, Poiln un Litaun*); S.S and the Sejurists and Labor Zionist Party *(Poale Zion)*.[48]

The political parties acted independently of the Kehilah from 1905 to 1917. It was all part of a complex process, not unique to Russia alone. The process ran parallel with efforts towards civic emancipation. In Russia, however, the emancipation was more of a pious dream than a reality, even after 1905. In spite of these difficulties, the Jewish people began to advance political claims and Dubnov argued "the core of nationality should have been separated from its heavy religious shell."[49] The process of secularization and separation of religions from all other activities, took on a highly complicated and involved form, fitting neither the previous epoch in which all activities were dominated by religious sanctions, nor the more modern version in which non-religious activities were separated from the control of the leadership of the synagogue.

Education presented a particularly serious problem up to the revolution. Each of the more prominent political parties began to take an interest in building its own educational facilities, which would have led to an enormous material burden. Therefore, compromises between the various political interests were effected. In the field of periodicals and newspapers, each group publishing its own paper or magazine, some in more than one language. For instance, among the Zionist-oriented periodicals there were, thirty-nine publications in Yiddish, by 1917, ten in Hebrew and three in the Russian language (Voskhod, Razsvet, Evreiski Mir).[50]

The following is a recapitulation of the Russian government's policies toward the Jews.

(1) In 1881 pogroms were, in the words of Minister Ignatev[51] "popular justice," while in 1905 they were officially called "patriotic demonstrations." The earlier pogroms were justified on economic grounds; namely, that the Jews exploited the inhabitants of the state and hence a *quid pro quo* was in order on various occasions as the government saw fit. The later pogroms were justified on political grounds. In 1905, the Russian people were said to have been taking revenge against the Jews for their part in the revolutionary movement. This was in fact admitted by V.K. Plehve to Dr. T. Herzl, the Zionist leader, in 1903, when the latter visited Russia. Plehve justified the government-directed pogroms by arguing that Jewish youth was actively participating in the Socialist movement, and hence this created a need to eradicate subversion within the Jewish population.[52] Thereafter, those charged with maintaining public order (the police and the army) were given permission to destroy Jewish resistance. During the October pogroms of 1905, the police and soldiers joined the mobs, and the Black Hundreds in perpetrating crimes of plunder, destruction of property and even murder.[53]

(2) The government's economic policies resulted in widespread poverty and restricted physical mobility of Jews to towns and cities in the Pale of Settlements. There were 5,189,401 Jews in Russia in 1897, or 4.13 percent of the population. The percentage of Jews living within the Pale was 93.93, as against 6.07 percent who lived outside. The territory of the Pale was one-twenty-third of the size of the territory of Russia. The proportion of the Jewish to the Christian population in the Pale was 11.46 percent, while outside the Pale it was 0.38 percent.[54]

On a whole, the Jewish population was extremely poor. Rosenthal, for example, makes reference to an article published in *Journal Du Nord* of 1892, which contained the following description:

"There are in Russia only ten thousand to fifteen thousand Jews who possess any certain means of existence. As to the masses they possess nothing; and they are poorer than the Christian populace, who at any rate own some land."[55]

The concentration of Jews into towns and cities began with the May Laws of 1882 and was continued during the next quarter of a century. The purpose of the policy was to isolate Jews further, and to force them into occupations where social intercourse with non-Jews was restricted. Of the over five million Jews in 1897, 500,986 or 13.2 percent were artisans. Among them the largest number were tailors (38.7 percent), followed by shoemakers (17 percent), carpenters (9.9 percent), metal workers (9.8 percent) building and ceramic trades (6.3 percent) and weavers and rope-makers (3.7 percent).[56]

In 1904, the number of artisans was about the same, while the number of Jewish factory workers was close to 45,000.[57] In an article written in 1906, Dubnov, analyzing the Marxist view of the economic position of Russian Jewry, defined their situation as follows:

"Economically, the Jewish nationality in Russia resembles at present a magnetic field which has two poles at the ends and a large "neutral line" in the middle. The upper bourgeoisie and the organized proletariat occupy only small positions at the two extreme poles at this time, and the economic center does not rest in them but in the middle line, in that great mass of artizans and petty traders who, according to their standard of living, should be counted with the proletariat."[58]

This large mass in the middle resulted from the economic restrictions imposed on the Jews by the government. It provided the reservoir for the increasingly large emigration to the West, which was part of Pobedonostsev's scheme for the solution of the Jewish question.

(3) Assimilation of Jews was also part of the same grand design of Pobedonostsev. There were two aspects to this policy of assimilation: baptism and russification. Both were forced upon Russian Jews, the latter policy much more successfully than the former. The demand for assimilation of Jews was not restricted to government policy, or to conservative elements within the ruling class. It was often expressed even by outstanding liberals, such as Yuzkov who, in 1901, wrote: "We do not take it upon ourselves to make the Jews into Russians, but we

want them to do it themselves." The publicist Struve is also quoted as saying: "For the good of Russia, I would want the Jews to assimilate. I believe it would be also to the advantage of the Jews."[59] But even those who were "assimilated" obtained no respite from discrimination. A report on the appointment of a rabbi in Ekaterinoslav described the social position of "assimilated" Jewish lawyers who, despite baptism, were excluded from Russian society and "willy-nilly had to take an interest in Jewish affairs." [60] The report then continued:

"They [the baptized Jews] had only succeeded in evading all the obstacles that the Russian law placed in the path of the intellectual Jew. It is not easy to say whom their sudden change insulted more, the Jews or the Christians. However, there was one obstacle that their change could not overcome — the social one. Russian society remained cold to them even after baptism."[61]

The policy of assimilation proved counter-productive during this period. The position of the Zionists grew stronger each year, and, by 1906, became the overriding influence within the Jewish community. This occurred despite the fact that since 1903, the Zionists were not allowed to hold meetings.[62] The intellectual and political strength of Russian Zionist leaders can also be judged from their dominant position within the world Zionist movement. During the so-called Uganda crisis, the Russian Zionists opposed the British government's offer to settle Jews in Uganda, re-established the unity of the movement and, in Russia, enthusiastically led strong campaigns for the revival of the Hebrew culture, writings in prose, poetry, theater (Habima) and newspapers. "It was clear to everyone," wrote Shmaryahu Levin, "that Russian Jewry, once emancipated, would take over the leadership of world Jewry."[63] The development of political affairs in Russia, however, took unanticipated turns. Notwithstanding the emancipation of Jews in 1917, these expectations never materialized.

(4) The 1907 coup and the declaration of war in 1914, froze the development of political activity among Russian Jews. The 1907 coup effectively limited the powers of the Duma and dealt a serious blow to

progressive and liberal elements. For all practical purposes, it also silenced the activity of Jewish political parties.

Shortly after the outbreak of the war, correspondence in Yiddish was prohibited and the publication of Yiddish newspapers and periodicals was banned.[64] The prohibition of the use of Hebrew characters in all publications on July 15, 1915, resulted in Jews remaining without any news and commentaries written by Yiddish journalists during the whole period of the war. In addition, Jews were again used as a scapegoat for military failures, and the government-supported newspapers presented Jews as "enemy agents disloyal to Russia."[65] The war disrupted the life of people in or near the war zones, including the mass of Jews concentrated in the western provinces. As a result of enemy operations, hundreds of thousands of people found themselves refugees on the roads leading east. This situation forced the government to "temporarily suspend" the enforcement of the laws, which restricted Jewish physical mobility to the Pale of Settlements. Jews were therefore allowed to resettle in the interior of Russia. The wartime conditions did have one positive aspect, in the otherwise gloomy picture. The Jewish communities organized a campaign of self-help for the refugees on a nation-wide scale. This revived somewhat the activities of the communal organs, and the February Revolution of 1917, found the Jewish communities active at least in some aspects of welfare, shelter and religious services.

Together with others, Jews enthusiastically welcomed the fall of the Tsar and, from the beginning, actively participated in the formation of a new democratic system. They had hopes of a new Russia consisting of a federation of free nations, enjoying full national and cultural autonomy. They were opposed from the outset by two powerful forces, the separatists among some of the territorial nationalities, and by the centralizing tendencies prevailing in the Bolshevik Party.

The creation of a democratic system alone held out great prospects for the now much smaller population of Jews in Russia. The abrogation of all disabilities and inequalities by the Provisional Government on March 20, 1917,[66] was expected. When the new decree was actually published, Jews were convinced that a new era of freedom had arrived. In the first few weeks, each day brought verification of newly bestowed freedoms. Jews were invited to participate in the administration of the new regime. The commission charged with the preparation of the decree of equality of all citizens before the law, had a former Jewish deputy of the Fourth Duma, L.M. Bramson, as one of its most active members. In fact, it was part of the Jewish draft proposals that Jews should not be specifically mentioned in the decree, but that the law be general in removing all disabilities of religion, creed or nationality. The Jewish draft proposals followed the policy established during the petition drive of the Jewish communities in 1904, when they demanded for all Russian nationalities the right of national-cultural self-determination.[67]

The pent-up forces within Russian Jewry burst with widespread activity in all areas considered vital to the growth of an autonomous national Jewish community. This was evident in the cultural and educational fields with the reappearance of a great number of dailies and periodicals, and in the political sphere with the emergence from the under-ground of Jewish political parties. The latter began a feverish round of activities in connection with the planned convocation of a representative national body, which would draft a political program. The spokesmen of all Jewish political parties, including the Bund, had accepted Dubnov's assertion that the Jews are a separate national group. Some differences in interpretation remained, particularly in regard to "the precise form and limits of national autonomy; on the links to the Jewish people outside the borders of Russia; and on the attitude to Zionism."[68] The attempts to assemble the all-Russian Jewish Congress proved abortive due to the November Revolution of 1917. Instead, the Jewish National Council was formed in the spring of 1918, to "safeguard the national political interests of our people in this land."[69] However, it never developed into the organization it was supposed to be. Therefore, ended the political aspirations of the Jewish nationality to have democratically elected representative organs, and the forces released by the February Revolution were soon effectively quenched.

CHAPTER III

THE SOVIET THEORY OF NATIONALITY AND THE JEWS

The following thoughts clearly explain Marx's misconception of the Jews from his essay, "The Jewish Question":

> "The German Jews seek emancipation. What kind of emancipation do they want? Civic, political emancipation.
>
> Bruno Bauer replies to them: In Germany no one is politically emancipated. We ourselves are not free. How then could we liberate you? You are egoists if you demand for yourselves, as Jews, a special emancipation."[70]

Jews were asking for equal democratic rights, along with other German subjects, but Marx, through his economic interpretation of history, saw this struggle as futile. According to him, nationalism was a divergence on the road to the inevitable Communist utopia — a utopia which posited that the class struggle was the only meaningful one, and that Communism was the final solution to man's alienation from man. Nationalism was viewed as part and parcel of this alienation. But herein lies his misconception of the Jewish question. While E. Fromm may be correct in stating in the foreword to Bottomore's edition of Karl Marx's writings that he was "discussing the difference between political emancipation and human emancipation."[71] Marx nevertheless chose to disregard the immediate inequality of Jews, and considered their demand a "special emancipation," calling them "egoists" if they persisted in demanding it.

Marx's discussion of the Jewish religion, his equating of Judaism with commercial activity, and Jewish nationality with the "nationality of the trader," have all been previously discussed by other writers.[72] Erich Fromm, commented that while Marx said some harsh words about what he thought was the Jewish religion, he also said some equally harsh words about the British shopkeepers, German philosophers and the Russians.[73] Marx completely disregarded the fact that the Jews, despite their heterogeneity produced by the Diaspora, were bound together by a common history and had acquired a group personality. Marx's concept was based on the Western experiences in nation-states, which did not face the problems of multinational countries. To Marx, a true internationalist was a proletarian of any state "who had no preference for any nation, and who was critical of all, never respecting the taboos of national feeling."[74] With the help of hindsight, it can be shown that in fact civil inequality, which existed as regards to German Jews at the time of Marx's observations, can be perpetuated, and even transferred into another social and political system. It is no surprise that Marx's authorship was used as late as 1968, to justify attacks on Judaism.[75]

Marx and Engels were aware of the force of nationalism in relations between nations, but as I have implied earlier, did not believe it could prevent the inevitable victory of the proletariat. The assumption was that capitalism will pave the way for Communism by leveling all national differences and bring about a "world wide international civilization."[76] This pillar of Communist faith was supported by Marxist tenets of disintegration of the capitalist state due to economic contradictions inherent in capitalism, and of a class struggle within each nation, which will cause, among other things, a realignment within the proletariat. This realignment with the proletariats of various nations, it was assumed, would overcome nationalism.

Marx and Engels based their theories on conditions and experiences, confined to Germany and Western Europe. But at the turn of the century, socialism penetrated deeply into Central and Eastern Europe, where the problem of national minorities was acute in the Austrian and Russian empires. It could not be disregarded, for it had to be considered and explained by the Socialists, as they preached their program. The problem was considered earlier in the Austro-Hungarian Empire, because the latter was an advanced political system at the time, having an early emergence of socialist political parties espousing their philosophy.

The Socialists had no problem in dealing with the existence of large states, which comprised one nationality, that is, people bound together by a common language, history and other common experiences. Marx

and Engels's view on the historical necessity to form large states was
accepted by their followers in Austria and Russia. The view that large
states,

> "... alone represent the normal organization of the ruling bour-
> geoisie in Europe, and which are also indispensable for the har-
> monious international co-operation of peoples, without which
> the rule of the proletariat is not possible ."[77]

This was accepted not only by Lenin and Stalin, but by Rosa
Luxemburg as well (who incidentally differed from them in other
aspects of interpretation of the Marxist theory). This acceptance of the
need for large states gave rise to another question: How do we accom-
modate the aspiration of small nations in Central and Eastern Europe
and still maintain the goal of a world-wide voluntary fusion of national
cultures into a proletarian culture?

The problem came up at the Bruenn Conference of the Austrian
Social Democrats, held in 1899. Two solutions to the question of
national minorities and their cultures were offered for consideration.
The first was based on the principle of *territorial* division into regional
units, along the ethnographic limits of each nationality. The second was
based on an *extraterritorial* national-cultural autonomy throughout the
empire, regardless of territorial divisions. Both accepted Marx's view of
the historical need to preserve the large state, in this case the Austro-
Hungarian monarchy. The Bruenn Congress accepted a compromise,
which proposed a new constitutional arrangement for Austria, and
which advocated transforming this country into a federation of nationalities. The Czech Social Democrats, strongly recommended that the
government of the historic Crown lands (Bohemia and Moravia) be in
the hands of Czech national bodies, democratically elected by the Czech
population. This was a recommendation which the Congress finally
accepted. The Austrian Social Democratic Party, was then reorganized
along national lines, and the Czechs later earned Lenin's epithet as the
"separatists in Austria," who he claimed, "destroyed the former unity
that existed between the Czech and German workers."[78]

The idea of extraterritorial or personal national-cultural autonomy was developed by Karl Renner and Otto Bauer — two Socialist theoreticians, who were fully aware of the particular problems facing minority nationalities in Austria. Their solution was based on a concept of nationality, which gave full priority to the nation over the state. The concept was based on the premise that a nation:

"… is the carrier of the new order, which is visualized … as a community of peoples … indestructible and undeserving of destruction…. Far from being unnational or antinational, it places nations at the foundation of its world structure."[79]

It is instructive to contrast this concept with Marx and Engels's view of the "anachronistic." Slav states whose "natural and inescapable destiny" was a process of "dissolution and absorption by their stronger neighbors."[80]

Marx and Engels were both wrong in expecting the disappearance of nationalism as a motivating political force.[81] The political history of the twentieth century is full of examples to support this view. Renner and Bauer saw it at the turn of the century, and argued "nationalism had to be faced directly, and the nation had to be recognized as a valuable and enduring form of social organization."[82] Therefore, "Social democracy proceeds not from existing states, but from live nations."[83] The first political party to accept the Austrian concept was the Bund. At its Fourth Congress, the Renner-Bauer plan was included in its platform declaring that "the concept of nationality is also applicable to the Jewish people."[84] Lenin shared Marx's view that the nation is a temporary phenomenon, "a specific historical category emerging from the economic necessities of rising capitalism," which will eventually "give way to a world community with a single culture and language."[85] He therefore rejected the Austrian concept in all its implications, particularly when it came to the idea of a federation, a necessary conclusion arising logically from the thesis "of nations at the foundation of a world structure." The Bund, on the other hand, demanded that "Russia should be transformed into a federation of nationalities. Each nationality, wherever it resided enjoying complete autonomy," and further that the "Russian Social Democratic Party be reconstructed on federal lines."[86] By 1901, the concept of national-cultural autonomy (a derivation of the Austrian thesis) was commonly accepted not only by members of the Bund, but by a large cross-section of the Jewish population, whether nationally diaspora oriented, Zionist or Orthodox. Therefore, it was quite natural to expect for the Bund, as a representative of the Jewish working class, to demand that the:

> "… Russian Social Democracy, with which it was affiliated, recognize the Bund as the sole representative of the Jewish proletariat in whatever part of Russia it lives and *whatever language it speaks*."[87]

The reference to "whatever language," indicates the view that the Jewish nationality does not require an exclusive language for purposes of identification. Lenin opposed the demand of the Bund that it be recognized as the sole representative of the Jewish working class, and it came as no surprise that "he was particularly insistent in rejecting national autonomy as a basis for party organization."[88] The demand that Jews be recognized as a nation, and the Bund as sole representative of the Jewish working class, was denounced by I.O. Martov, then editor of the Party organ *Iskra*, as "nationalistic, un-Marxian and completely impractical."[89] This denunciation was followed later in almost similar language by L. Trotsky and G.V. Plekhanov, who were both ready to expel the Bund from the Party. Lenin, who also participated in the debates, mockingly asserted:

> "The Bundists need now only to work out the idea of a separate nationality of Russian Jews, whose language is Yiddish and whose territory is — the Pale of Settlement."[90]

The truth remained that despite their heterogeneity on many issues, the Jews considered themselves as a nation. Though not a necessary component of their nationality, Yiddish had virtually become the universal language of Jews, not only within the Pale, but in most of Eastern Europe. In addition to the claim to recognition of a distinct Jewish nation, there were other doctrinal differences between the Bund and Lenin. Among them was the subordination of national struggle to the class struggle, an assertion which the Bund would not accept. In this opposition, the Bund was not alone within Russian Jewry. "We will support the position," said Dubnov, "that the class principle must be subordinated to the national principle."[91] The conflicting views on this fundamental issue between the Bund on one hand, and Lenin on the other, could not be clearer.

The Jews were not the only ones, among Russia's national minorities, to present similar views on the Renner-Bauer formula. Caucasian socialists also supported the Bund. Lenin, in answer to Armenian demands for a federal system in Russia, and the introduction of cultural autonomy, objected:

"It is not the business of the proletariat to preach federation and national autonomy ... which unavoidably led to the demand for the establishment of an autonomous class state."[92]

By 1912, even some Mensheviks began to advocate national-cultural autonomy. In view of this, Lenin commissioned J.V. Stalin to study the Austrian concept, which was based on the extra-territorial national-cultural autonomy. Stalin's study, later published in his *Marxism and the National Question* (1913),[93] was perhaps the most systematic essay in classical Marxist literature on Jewish nationality. Pipes referred to it in critical terms when he wrote of Stalin's efforts; "they hardly fulfilled" Lenin's expectations "to refute the Austrian ideas, which were gaining prevalence among Russian Marxists."[94] Stalin's essay consisted of three main parts, the first of which dealt with the concept of the nation, which Stalin defined as a "historically evolved, stable community arising on the foundation of a common language, territory, economic life, and psychological makeup, manifested in a community of culture."[95] Referring, in particular, to Jews, Stalin asked the following rhetorical question:

"... what ... national cohesion can there be ... between the Georgian, Daghestanian, Russian and American Jews? ... if there is anything common to them left it is their religion, their common origin and certain relics of national character. But how can it be seriously maintained that petrified religious rites and fading psychological relics affect the 'fate' of these Jews more powerfully than the living social, economic and cultural environment that surrounds them?" [96]

Stalin was of the opinion that the Jews in Russia were heading for inevitable assimilation. The struggle against this trend was reflected in the demand of the Bund for recognition of a Jewish nation and in Jewish cultural autonomy. Stalin, as can be seen from his definition of the concept of the nation, denied that Jews are a nation and his view was primarily based on lack of territorial concentration, and also a lack of "a large and stable stratum associated with the soil." [97] In other words, it was a lack of a substantially large peasant class. The peasants were to form the base of the people, a "framework", and were to act as a "national market." Jews in Russia did not have this base, and to complete his analysis of Russian Jews, Stalin further interpreted the results of their dispersion among other nationalities, as giving them particular social functions. For example, Jews as a "rule serve 'foreign nations' in respect to language and so forth." [98] With the definition of Jews, which implied a denial of nationality, and the interpretation of their social functions on the eve of the First World War, Russian Jews were, according to Stalin, destined to inevitable assimilation.

Pipes divided Lenin's approach to the national problem into three phases: from 1897 to 1913, from 1913 to 1917, and from 1917 to 1923. In the second phase, from 1913 to 1917, Lenin developed a plan for the utilization of minority movements in Russia and abroad, and for this purpose, devoted the last two years preceding World War I to research on the nationality problem. He considered the concept of "national culture" as erroneous from a Marxist point of view, and, with reference to the Jewish national culture, he wrote:

"Jewish national culture is the slogan of the rabbis and the bourgeoisie — the slogan of our enemies. But there are other elements of Jewish culture and in the whole history of Jewry. Out of some ten and a half million Jews in the world, a little more than half live in Galicia and Russia, backward and semi-barbarian countries which keep the Jews by force in the position of an outlawed caste." [99]

Lenin consistently expressed his view that culture could only have a class character, and in classical Marxist vein asserted: "The toilers can talk only of an international culture of the universal worker movement." [100] He also opposed the federal principle, whether within the party or in the state. During the first phase, 1903 to be exact, Lenin agreed with the principle of self-determination, but ten years later felt it ought to be reinterpreted due to its vagueness. "As a statement of principle," wrote Pipes, "it was open to divergent interpretations. It could mean national territorial autonomy, cultural autonomy of a territorial or extraterritorial kind, or the establishment of federal relations." [101]

By 1913, Lenin thought he had found the solution. He therefore defined the principle to mean, "political self-determination, in the sense that it gives right to separation and creation of an independent government." "People who did not desire to take advantage of this right," wrote Pipes, "could not ask from the state for any preferential treatment, such as the establishment of federal relations, or the granting of extraterritorial cultural autonomy." [102]

While the question of self-determination did not affect the position of Jews in the same sense as the term was reinterpreted by Lenin, it seemed to be a consistent and logical explanation of Marxism, and most useful for winning support among the many national minorities of Russia. Jews could not hope, under this interpretation, for a development of their national culture as they understood it. Their views and program conflicted with Lenin's and Stalin's theories on national culture. Jews desired a broad national and cultural autonomy, while Lenin, "like most Marxists, desired the eventual transformation of the Russian Empire into a national state, in which the minorities would assimilate and adopt the Russian tongue." [103] The conflict between the Bolshevik doctrine and the Jews was therefore to inevitably persist.

CHAPTER IV

THE BOLSHEVIKS IN POWER

On attaining power, Lenin was faced with enormous problems, the most important being the preservation of the unity of the state. In addition to the two opposing camps, the Bolsheviks and the Whites, there was a third group: the national minorities, generally bent on exploiting the difficulties of the Bolshevik government for their own purposes. It was imperative for Lenin to harness these minority forces in many crucial areas of the country. Thus temporary concessions, which ran counter to Lenin's theoretical theses, were made by the Bolsheviks to the minority groups. These concessions were quickly reversed as the war situation changed, and became more favorable to the Bolsheviks. Good examples of this point includes the Treaty with Georgia, and its reoccupation by the Red Army ten months later; and the promises made to the Iugushi, when they alone stood between the opposing Cossacks and the territory under formal Bolshevik control. In both instances, written promises were broken without any regard to either ethical aspects or the feelings of respective minority groups.

The Jews were a problem *sui generis*. They were not considered a political force strong enough to endanger the position of the government, and they could in no way affect the territorial unity of the state. The Jewish people awoke from a nightmare which lasted several hundred years. As chapter two has briefly outlined, between 1905 and 1917, they made — as a collective group — enormous strides to enter the twentieth century, not as a backward people, but as a politically mature people. In all fields of cultural endeavor and political organization they transformed themselves from an oppressed group, to a people intent to live freely as a national group. Thus, when Lenin came to power he was faced with the fact that the Jewish people were bent on achieving cultural autonomy, including control over their whole educational system.

Among the Jewish people, the most active organized groups were the Zionists and Bundists, both long considered by Lenin as reactionaries and separatists. Therefore, Lenin understood the Jewish question to be:

"… The Jewish question is this exactly: assimilation or separateness? And the idea of a "Jewish nationality" is manifestly reactionary, not only when put forward by its consistent partizans (the Zionists), but also when put forward by those who try to make it agree with the ideas of Social Democracy (the Bundists). The idea of a Jewish nationality is in conflict with the interests of the Jewish proletariat, for, directly or indirectly, it engenders in its ranks a mood hostile to assimilation, a "ghetto" mood." [104]

The Zionists and the Bundists were not only the most active groups, but they were also the most numerous as well. The Zionists, for instance, had at this time, 1,200 local organizations with a membership of 300,000. This was by far the largest and best-organized political movement among the Jews. [105]

This political reality, existing among the Jewish people in Soviet Russia, was a strong contributory factor to Lenin's reversal of his original stand, and to his inclusion of a Jewish nationality, among the nationalities of Soviet Russia. Though there were previous indications of a change, especially from 1914 onwards (see Lenin's draft of a bill on nationality for the Bolshevik delegation in the Duma); a resolution adopted at the Tenth Congress of the Communist Party, specifically mentioned Jews in a list of examples of nationalities and national minorities. [106] This move on the part of the Communists was a tactical manoeuvre. The strained political situation at the time conflicted with the growing cultural and political awareness of many other nationalities in the country, and forced these temporary concessions from the Bolsheviks. "Realist that he [Lenin] was," commented Baron, "he did not mind reversing his previous stand and including the Jews in the new declaration of the rights of nationalities (November 15, 1917)." [107]

The revised stand appeared to take note of reality, but it was not followed by a genuine rethinking of the doctrinal position. This may have

been due to a lack of interest, or more likely to the fact that more press-
ing problems of the state had to be considered first. It remains a fact,
however, that neither Lenin nor Stalin published anything during this
period, which served to indicate a basic doctrinal change on this matter. The special appeal addressed to "All Muslim Toilers of Russia and
the East" serves as an example of the Bolshevik strategy. The appeal
assured the Muslims:

> "Your beliefs and usages, your national and cultural institutions are
> henceforth free and inviolable, [and] organize your life freely and
> without hindrance. You have a right to do this, [because] your
> rights like those of all peoples of Russia are protected b the entire
> might of the Revolution and its organs." [108]

The Bolsheviks really had no such intention of allowing the organization of "national life freely and without hindrance." This appeal
made under duress on November 20, 1917, in no way affected their
doctrinal position. Some five years later, Lenin was quoted as saying to
a Jewish correspondent of the *Manchester Guardian:*

> "... the experience of the preceding five years had fully con-
> vinced the Soviet Government that the only way to eliminate
> nationalist strife was to offer maximum satisfaction to the aspira-
> tions of all nationalities." [109]

What this "maximum satisfaction" meant to Soviet Jews, as individuals and as a collective, will be analyzed on the following pages.

A Commissariat for Jewish National Affairs was created by the
Bolshevik leaders, shortly after coming to power. The Commissariat
was a special section within the People's Commissariat for Nationality
Affairs, and its task was to establish "the dictatorship of the proletariat
in the Jewish streets,"[110] or, in other words, to restructure the existing
complex organizational and social framework of Jewish communal
activities along Bolshevik party lines.

To assist and direct all these activities of the Commissariat of Jewish
National Affairs, a special section of the Party was established to

"modernize the cultural, political and economic life of a national minority, while preserving its ethnic identity."[111] This attempt met with general hostility from the Jewish people.

Among the first steps of the new regime was a publication, under the signatures of V.I. Ulianov (Lenin) and Joseph Dzugashvili (Stalin), of a "Declaration of the Rights of the Russian People."[112] This was followed fourteen months later, on August 8, 1918, by a "Decree of the Council of People's Commissars on the Uprooting of the Anti-Semitic Movement." The publication of the decree under the signature of Lenin and the Secretary of the Council of People's Commissars, N. Gorbunov, placed "pogromists and pogrom-agitators" outside the law, and instructed all Soviet deputies to "take uncompromising measures to tear the anti-Semitic movement out by the roots."[113] Both these measures announced the beginning of a new era in which legislative policy would follow the direction of one political party, though insofar as Jewish affairs were concerned, some limited pluralism was tolerated for a few years as a matter of expediency.[114]

The Declaration, published after the Second Congress of Soviets in October 1917, contained four principles on which the Council of People's Commissars planned its policy in regard to all nationalities. The first two were related to nationalities living in their own territories, but the third and fourth principles were also applicable to Jews. The first principle, called for the equality and sovereignty of the nations of Russia; while the second principle, spoke of the right of the nations of Russia to free self-determination, including separation, and the formation of independent states. The third principle, advocated: "The removal of every and any national and national-religious privilege and restriction," therefore, indicating quite clearly that the authors of the Declaration were well aware of the influence existing between the national element and religion. A resolution adopted by a conference of Jewish educators in Minsk was cited as evidence of this influence. The resolution spoke of "the difficulty of secularizing Jewish education, [because] Jewish religion [had] penetrated all aspects of the Jewish way of life."[115] The fourth principle, referred to the "free development of national minorities and ethnographic groups.[116] How this fourth principle was to be interpreted by the Party was not long in forthcoming.

As a first step, a resolution was proposed at the First Conference of the Jewish Sections of the Communist Party in Moscow to abolish the communal institution, known as Kehilah, and the Central Board of Jewish communities. The Conference took place in October 1918, and the final draft of the resolution was approved in April 1919. The resolution became law four months later, on August 5. 1919. The delegates to the Conference represented thirteen regional units: thirty-one of the delegates were communists and thirty-three were handpicked "impartial delegates."[117] The decision to abolish the Kehilah and the Central Board was published in a decree signed by Stalin and Samuel Agurski, Assistant Head of the Commissariat of Jewish National Affairs. In view of the historic importance of this step, it may be useful to recall that the resolution to dissolve the Kehilot in its final draft accused the Jewish communities and their Central Board of:

(a) serving as rallying points for undisguised enemies of the interests of the working class and the achievements of the October Revolution;

(b) pursuing an injurious policy directed at dimming the class consciousness of the Jewish working masses; and

(c) bringing up the growing Jewish generation in an anti-proletarian spirit.[118]

With the dissolution in August 1919 of the traditional Jewish institution of the Kehilot and the dismissal of democratically elected organs, Soviet Jewry lost its last independent national organization. The dissolution of the Kehilot was an immediate and serious blow to the Jewish community, because these institutions served on a local communal level as centres for most of the activities of the Jewish community. From that date forward, Jews dispersed across the territories of the Soviet Union and remained without a representative body of their own.

Just prior to the dissolution of the Kehilah, the activities of the Jewish community had undergone vast expansion. Under the umbrella of the Kehilah, functioned a school system with ancillary cultural and educational activities. The exigencies of the unsettled times and civil war, with its disruption of public services, added new burdens to the responsibilities of the Kehilah. Among them were soup kitchens, shelter and health aid. Therefore, the Kehilah was to a great extent an autonomous organ of the Jewish people, serving its needs, as though it were a government agency on a local level. The abolition of the Kehilah exposed the most vulnerable part of the body of Jewish communal strength and way of life. From this time forward, the individual Jew depended exclusively on his Jewish national consciousness, and at times, was supported by the use of his mother tongue, Yiddish.

The reaction of Jews to the abolition of the Kehilah was bitter, and the community resorted to passive resistance as a protest. Both sets of agencies, the Commissariat for Jewish National Affairs and the Jewish Sections of the Party, began to recruit personnel, and found great difficulty in hiring qualified staff.[119] " ... when the communists took over," wrote Epstein, "and had to establish their power in cities in the Ukraine and Belorussia, thickly populated by Jews, they had practically no one to fill the local Soviet apparatus, not to speak of their local units."[120] The new agencies possessed no personnel speaking Yiddish, and the daily paper, the *Warhayt* (Truth), published by the Yevsektsiia, had to use outside translators for the material supplied by the Party. Epstein maintained that "at first neither the Yevsektsiia nor the Commissariat had any line of communication with the Jewish people."[121] The top officers of the Commissariat, S.M. Dimanshtein and his chief assistant, Samuel Agurski, arrived in Russia only after the first revolution.

The mass of Russian Jews continued to actively participate in organizations of their own choice, which were barely tolerated by the authorities. This period of tolerance on the part of the Party and the government, was due to external and internal difficulties faced by the new Bolshevik regime, and was not to last very long. The "Yevsektsia," wrote Schechtman, "was increasingly dismayed by the apparent semi-tolerance of the Soviet authorities and urged total proscription and liquidation of Zionism."[122] This situation prevailed from July 1920, continuing well beyond 1922.

In summary, it can be stated that during the greater part of the first five-year period of the Bolshevik regime, there was no noticeable consistency

in the policies adopted toward the Jewish minority. The local government offices, at times, relented to Yevsektsia's prodding, but at other
times, resisted it or declined to give acquiescence to many of its
demands. During this period, some of the important daily tasks, formerly
performed by the Kehilah, such as social welfare and education, were
either neglected or completely abandoned.

Rothenberg is right in asserting that the "Jewish *religious* leaders had
not made any attempts to oppose the new government"[123] The same
could equally be said of Jewish *political* leaders. What did the term
"opposition to the new government" mean in those days? An effective
opposition could only have been a military opposition. There was no
means to oppose the government of that day by methods and processes
used in parliamentary systems. And, of course, there was no Jewish military force among the interventionist forces. It was a general hostility
towards the regime, among the declassed strata of the Jewish population, mainly because of religious and socio-economic reasons.[124] There
was also a noticeable resentment among the Jewish masses, because
they had lost the Kehilah, their "frontline defence," which protected
them from arbitrary actions of the Tsar, the Black Hundreds, and hope-
fully, the Bolshevik regime. The perimeter and centre fell in one dramatic swoop. The resulting consequences of this step were much better foreseen and understood by Jewish communists than by the
non-Jewish leaders of the government. Step by step the Yevsektsiia
began to erode the cultural heritage of the Jewish people, by a process
defined as "dehistorization."[125]

What did the Jewish resistance consist of in those days? First, Jews did
not join the Communist Party with any enthusiasm.[126] Neither did they
volunteer for services within the local Soviet administration, and many
former Jewish functionaries of the Jewish socialist parties refused to join
despite pressures and threats used by the Jewish Sections of the Party. Only
much later, after some pogroms by the opposing military forces under the
command of former Tsarist generals and admirals, did Jews in larger
numbers join the local Soviets and the Party. Second, Jews continued some
limited educational and cultural activities in the special agricultural centres in which Jewish youth was being prepared for emigration to

Palestine. Third, the three Zionist parties continued their activities "virtually unimpeded" through 1918, and the first several months of 1919.[127]

"Palestine weeks" were held in various Russian cities, with thousands of "enthusiastic Jews participating." The British Balfour Declaration was hailed as the "first step to international recognition of a Jewish Palestine." J.A. Naiditsch, Vice-President of the Moscow Jewish Community, concluded that "the Jewish Commissariat, which at first proclaimed the fight against Zionism ... as one of its chief tasks, has up to now accomplished nothing of consequence."[128] The Zionists, alone among the Jewish parties, tried at least on two different occasions to secure official recognition by the new regime and to establish their legal status. Where they failed, the Jewish Section of the Communist Party succeeded. By creating internal fights within the parties, by pitting one group against another, and creating general disruption, the Jewish Section managed to impose its will and control. It succeeded by tactics previously used by Lenin in 1903, primarily against the Bund, but later against others. Had the Zionists infiltrated the Jewish Sections, their attempts at a *modus vivendi* with the new regime may have had a better chance of success at this early date.

The fact that Zionists submitted an application for legalization of their organized activities stands as proof that other alternative roads were also sought. As late as in the fall of 1925, Zionist leaders submitted a memorandum to Peter Smidovich, then acting head of VTsIK (All-Russian Central Executive Committee), outlining Zionist aims. A special session of the VTsIK "discussed the request (for authorization of emigration to Palestine) at considerable length, but inconclusively, the Zionists were advised to submit a project for a legalized emigrationary society."[129] The Jewish Section of the Communist Party intervened, the executive committee listened, and the attempt by Zionists to establish agreement with the regime failed.

That was the situation of the Jewish people in Soviet Russia in the first five years of the regime. The activities of the Jewish Sections contributed to the development of a new, secular Yiddish language, which for a time was used in schools, in Jewish courts, and, in some cases, in mixed local soviets. Yiddish, was one of the official languages in

Belorussia. It was also the language used in the official paper of the Party, and in communications with the Party's Jewish members. In general, Yiddish was an essential component of the Jewish nationality. The zealots of the Jewish Section, aimed to create a concept of a completely new language "national in form and proletarian in content or culture." By 1923, the Jewish Section attained its main goals: it completed the "revolution in the Jewish street"; established a new "proletarian" Yiddish language with a threadbare connection to its former rich literary sources; and destroyed all traditional Jewish institutions and Jewish political parties.

Having completed its preliminary tasks, the Jewish Section now intensified its emphasis on attaining a higher stage of development; namely, the assimilation of Jews "into one common socialist culture." Therefore, at the Sixth Conference of the Jewish Sections in Moscow, Maria Y. Frumkina was quoted as saying:

> "... very likely the process of assimilation will engulf all national minorities in the cities.... Considering the probability of such assimilation, we must, by our approach, indoctrinate the Jewish workers and leaders *not to judge each particular activity from the standpoint of national self-preservation*, but rather from its usefulness to socialist reconstruction."[130]

This development toward denationalization was not unanimously supported among the leaders of the Jewish Sections. It was also not consistent with the efforts of some of the Soviet leaders, particularly Michael I. Kalinin, then Chairman of the Presidium of the Central Executive Committee of the U.S.S.R. In a much cited speech to the first congress of the Ozet[131] on November 17, 1926, Kalinin formulated his views, which were quite contrary to those stated by Frumkina:

> "The Jewish people is confronted by a great problem, the maintenance of its own nationality, and for this it is necessary to transform a substantial portion of the Jewish population into a compact, settled, rural population numbering at least some hundreds

of thousands. It is only in such conditions that the Jewish masses will be able to hope for their future existence as a nationality."[132]

The efforts to maintain Jewish nationality were obviously inconsistent with the long-range plans to assimilate and fuse Jews "into a common socialist culture." Both trends were visible for a number of years, from the early twenties to perhaps the end of 1934, at the time of the assassination of Kirov. Part of the activity to maintain a distinct Jewish nationalit, was always hidden in the efforts to create new or enlarge existing compact Jewish settlements, and eventually led to a plan to establish a territory for the Jewish nationality. Therefore, with the financial and professional help of the Agrojoint, Jewish agricultural settlements were established in several republics. Kalinin addressed himself to the "national feeling of the Jewish capitalists" abroad, when he appealed to them for financial support. An indication of the scope of these efforts can be shown from the following: toward 1929, the total sum of all expenditures on agricultural settlement of Jews in the Soviet Union came to 22.5 million rubles, of which 16.7 million were provided by Jewish organizations abroad.[133] Jewish capitalists and American trade unions, responded to the appeal with 74.2 percent of the budget. In 1929, some 220,000 Jews were estimated in farming settlements.

A change in policy began with a general process of "de-kulakization" in Jewish farming settlements, and soon little was left of the Crimean colonies. Then came the Birobidzhan project, which was established by a decree of the Presidium of the Central Executive Committee on March 28, 1928. It was hailed as a constructive contribution to a policy, which aimed at creating a compact Jewish national territory inhabited by a Jewish rural population. Kalinin expected a Jewish farming population of "at least some hundreds of thousands," so that the "Jewish masses would be able to hope for their future existence as a nationality."[134] The arguments against the project offered by Jews, were both objective and subjective in nature. Many of the objective arguments took the form of questioning the choice of territory, its strategic location, and its climate. But Jews also recalled that the Uganda project of some years previously was firmly declined by the

leaders of Russian Jewry, because Uganda was not the Jewish homeland, and only emigrating to Eretz Israel (Palestine) would satisfy them.
They were therefore prepared to await the time when such an opportunity became available rather than resettle in new Soviet territory. The
project was timed to proceed when other processes within the Party
progressed in the opposite direction. In February 1930, as part of a general reorganization of the Party, the Jewish Sections were abolished.

What official Soviet documents are available, mostly in the works of
former leaders of the Commissariat for Jewish National Affairs, deal
with the aims of the project rather than with the reasons for its failure.
Just before the Jewish Sections were abolished, efforts were undertaken
by them to "modernize" Jewish life by the arbitrary establishment of
new institutions to serve as visible expressions of a formal break with
previous traditions. Successful attempts were made to establish purely
Jewish Soviets and a new type of Jewish court. But all these changes
were looked upon by Jews as being hostile to the interests and the
maintenance of a distinct Jewish culture and nationality. The courts, for
instance, were used to "wean away the Jews from their ingrained habit
to go to rabbinical courts, considered as enemies of the people."[135]

The Jewish people emerged at the end of the first decade of Soviet
rule, integrated as individuals into the structure of the Soviet economy.
As a group, they were geographically dislocated from the traditional con-
centrations in Belorussia and the Ukraine. Part of this great move was
due to a personal choice to leave the villages for cities, but, in general, the
policy was identical to that created for the majority of Soviet peoples.
The move into cities had a denationalizing effect on Jews, and the trend
could not be prevented because the Jews had no institutions available to
them to do so. It soon became an almost impossible task to rebuild the
now loose group of individuals into a cohesive distinct national and cultural entity. The effects of this policy were perhaps more pernicious and
the results more lasting with the Jewish people, because first, the Jewish
Sections supported and executed this policy of dislocation. Secondly,
individual Jews dispersed among majorities of another culture and soon
began to lose their linguistic and spiritual heritage, which they were able
to previously retain in their former homes.

What happened to Soviet Jews was not accidental. It was not assimilation, because assimilation implied not only the will to be absorbed, but an acceptance by the absorbing society or nationality to facilitate this assimilation. "The census of 1926," wrote Nove and Newth, "is both comprehensive and fully detailed, and it remains our main source of information for the early period. The census of 1939, was never published in full, however, its findings were of course rendered to a major extent obsolete by the onset of the war...."[136] There is no accurate statistical data available for this period, and it appears that Jews as a minority group, temporarily lost any formal expression by which the cohesiveness of a national group could be judged. Hitler's anti-Jewish program may have effectively contributed to stop the trend to assimilation.

The thirties were the years of purges in the Soviet Union. The assassination of Kirov in December 1934, resulted in mass prosecutions of prominent communists, including Jews, suspected of disloyalty to Stalin. With the exception of Ozet's official periodical *Tribuna,* only the Yiddish language newspaper *Emes* survived the thirties. In January 1938, the *Tribuna* was discontinued and *Emes* suppressed. The purges destroyed some leaders of all nationalities, but in the case of Jews, the destruction went much further. "The Great Purge," wrote Schwarz, "virtually terminated the organized life of the Jewish group as a recognized cultural and ethnic minority."[137] When, for instance, journalists were purged, they were not replaced by others, and their newspapers were discontinued. This also happened in all fields of cultural endeavor.

In addition to *Tribuna* and *Emes* (Moscow), authorities discontinued the papers *Oktiabr* (Minsk) and *Shtern* (Kharkov). All works in Yiddish devoted to the history of the Jewish working-class movement, were confiscated and taken out of libraries.[138] The Jewish institutes attached to the Academies of Sciences in Kiev and Minsk, were closed. It was at this time, too, that the activities of the American Agrojoint and ORT were discontinued, and their local representatives arrested and liquidated.[139]

Jewish Communists suffered heavily in the 1938 liquidation of Party officials, who had fallen in disfavor with the dictator Stalin. Many who were active in the Jewish Sections of the Party, the Commissariat and in various educational, cultural and scientific fields, were shot. Among the leading Jewish Communist luminaries who lost their lives were: S. Dimanshtein, former head of the Commissariat of Jewish National Affairs; M. Litvakov, for sixteen years editor of *Emes*; former Bund leaders, "Esther" Frumkin, A. Weinstein and M. Rafes (leading the work of the Jewish Sections); Jacob Levin (one of the architects of the Birobidzhan project), and the literary critic T. Tsinberg, whose ten-volume history of Jewish literature was sent abroad just before his liquidation.[140]

CHAPTER V

ORIGIN OF THE JEWISH ANTI-FASCIST COMMITTEE

One of the consequences of the 1939 Non-Aggression Pact, was the substantial addition made to the Jewish population in Soviet Russia. There was at that time, a large population of Jews in the newly annexed territories of eastern Poland, western Ukraine and western Belorussia. With the further annexation of the Baltic States, Bukovina and Bessarabia in 1940, the increase became even more substantial.

The estimates of the increase varied from fifty to seventy percent, but this large discrepancy can be explained by a number of difficulties which faced the demographer. One of these was the difficulty involved in defining "who is a Jew." During the Tsarist period, and particularly from the 1897 census onwards, a Jew was this person registered in the Kehilah. A Jew, who by religion, was a Catholic or Greek Orthodox, ceased to be a Jew for the purposes of the census, though he may have been considered as such in terms of social acceptance. Secondly, in the Soviet Union, a person declared his nationality during census time, and his declaration was then considered sufficient for the purposes of compiling nationality figures for the country. This fact was substantially altered by a decree of the Central Executive Committee and the Council of People's Commissars on December 27, 1932, which created a domestic passport system.[141] Since then, the simple biological fact of being born of Jewish parents was the determining factor. Thirdly, the Baltic States and the two provinces of Rumania, had different methods of compiling nationality. This further created discrepancies in population estimates, when these territories were annexed to the Soviet Union by 1940.

With an estimated increase to their population from 1.8 million to 2 million, Russian Jews numbered approximately 5 million by 1940.[142] This was the official figure quoted by the Soviet Jewish leaders of that period, and up to 1943, and it was still being used in Jewish population estimates.[143] Even as late as 1944, during my negotiations with the Jewish Anti-Fascist Committee, this figure of five million, still remained the official population estimate of Soviet Jewry.[144] Disregarding the discrepancies in numbers, the fact still remained that this large infusion of religious and nationally conscious Jews with all their cultural and social organizations, had a tremendous revitalizing effect on Soviet Jewry.

From 1939 to 1941, Soviet Jewry was isolated from the outside world. Due to the previous series of purges, the community lived in fear and terror and consequently its cohesiveness deteriorated. When Molotov signed the 1939 Non-Aggression Pact with Hitler's Germany, a complete censorship was imposed on all news of Nazi atrocities, against Jews in Germany and in German-occupied territories. This news blackout on Nazi policy against the Jewish people had tragic consequences for Soviet Jewry, as well as for the Soviet population. Isaac Deutscher, the biographer of Stalin, attributed this policy to one of Stalin's personality traits. "You had, therefore," wrote Deutscher, "that very curious phenomenon that throughout the Second World War the Soviet press hardly ever mentioned Auschwitz and Maidanek.[145] Deutscher recorded that the "resulting confusion" and "tragic consequences could have been avoided," if the truth from Germany was publicly known. As an example, he pointed to the confusion and ignorance among Soviet Jewry:

"... When, in 1942 the Soviet government offered to evacuate the Taganrog Jews before the advancing Nazi armies, they refused to move: they did not believe that the German nation, the nation of Goethe and Beethoven ... the nation of Marx and Engels could possibly be guilty of such enormities towards the Jews as the Soviet authorities were telling them it was."[146]

Therefore, concluded Deutscher, "The Jews disbelieved Stalin's propaganda, even when that propaganda was true." History records, of course, the mass slaughter of the Jews of Taganrog. Only a few escaped or were evacuated in time to prevent a complete liquidation. Goldberg described a conversation he had with the Yiddish poet David Hofstein, who told him of his uncle, formerly living in a small place near Kiev, "who, along with a few other elders of the town, went forth to meet the invading Nazis with the traditional bread and salt. They were shot on the spot."[147] There was evidence of this ignorance in many other instances, but perhaps the most telling is contained in a Nazi military document from Belorussia, dated July 1941:

> "The Jews are strikingly ill-informed about our attitude toward them and about the treatment Jews are receiving in Germany or in Warsaw, *places after all not too remote from them*. If they were not, they could scarcely ask whether we in Germany treat Jews differently from other citizens." [148]

Goldberg prefaced his documentation by querying: "How could Jews anywhere, as late as 1941, have been so ignorant about Nazi persecutions and the sinister designs against Jews?" His own answer only partly explained the Soviet government's attitude. Goldberg believed that this immoral policy, which caused a great many people to be caught in a trap not of their own making, "was just part of an avowed cynical policy of the ends justifying the means. The Soviet leaders did not hesitate to suppress the news ... whenever they thought it served their purpose."[149]

It is suggested that while this policy may have been a concession to dormant anti-Jewish feelings in the population, which was fanned and exploited by wartime propaganda, it was nevertheless not focused against Jews alone. Perhaps the most telling evidence of the Soviet government's cynicism in this matter, was the wholesale handing over of known German anti-Fascist leaders to the waiting arms of the Gestapo at the historic bridge of Brest Litovsk.[150] Some attribute this particular aspect of Stalin's policy to his personality. Deutscher called it an "aspect of contempt and distrust,"[151] when he referred to later Soviet attempts to minimize or completely ignore Jewish losses at the hands of the Nazis. A more plausible argument was that this attitude was part of a general policy not to do anything, which might affect

the cooperation between Hitler and Stalin. An inkling of this general
policy, can perhaps be gleaned from an article in *Bezbozhnik* of May
1940, in which a recently returned correspondent from Nazi
Germany argued that the Nazi attack on the Jewish religion was the
principal achievement of the Third Reich. It was, the correspondent
continued, therefore the duty of Soviet atheists to assist Nazi
Germany in their fight against religion.[152]

Whatever the degree of influence Jews from the annexed territories
had on the life of Soviet Jews, it progressively diminished during the
short period of Soviet rule. Immediately after annexation, existing
institutions were allowed to continue for a few weeks, but shortly
thereafter, the Red Army personnel were replaced by civilian officials
and officers from the People's Commissariat of Internal Affairs
(N.K.V.D.). Both began measures to integrate the new citizens into the
Soviet system and to restructure their society, along the lines of the
Soviet model. Jewish writers, bowing to the party line, visited the new
communities and assisted them in their adjustment. Soviet Yiddish
writers, assisted the local Yiddish authors by helping them to find mar-
kets for their writings, and by introducing them to the Soviet literary
world. Early in 1941, Zelik Akselrod, a poet from Minsk, had a meeting in Kaunas with a select group of the local Jewish intelligentsia. He
revealed to the meeting that "attempts would be made to close down
the Yiddish schools, and he indicated that the only way to prevent these
attempts, were by categorical demands by parents for the continuation
of Jewish education for their children."[153] After this meeting, Akselrod
mysteriously "disappeared," and he was never seen again. The N.K.V.D.
came to the new territories with lists of "undesirable and untrustwor-
thy" elements. Not long afterwards, leaders of all Jewish parties, communal bodies and various cultural institutions, were arrested and
deported to Siberia. The Jewish school system, which had started to
prepare the groundwork for full utilization of Yiddish in all its teaching activities was dissolved, all within one year.[154]

Just before the German attack on the Soviet Union, the Communist
world suffered intense divisions and internal convulsions. To many
Soviet and foreign Communists, the cooperation with Nazi Germany
was an incredible and morally indefensible arrangement. The Slovak,

Vlado Clementis, and many other foreign Communists, opposed the pact, and resigned from the Party. The Soviet academic, Lena Shtern, asked her Party colleagues many probing questions. She told Ehrenburg: "A responsible comrade explained to me it was a marriage of convenience." Ehrenburg's cryptic reply to her was timely: "Such a marriage can produce off spring,"[155] and as he further commented:

> "Eight years later Lena Shtern personally experienced the correctness of her diagnosis: she was arrested with the other active members of the Jewish Anti-Fascist Committee; fortunately she survived."[156]

To many Communists, this "unholy" alliance between the Soviets and the Nazis was unexplainable from an ideological point of view. As a consequence, serious divisions of thought occurred among Communist intellectuals. Ehrenburg related his own experiences on the matter:

> "There were also some writers and journalists who said that I did not think like a Soviet citizen, I had lived too long in France, had grown attached to that country and was 'laying it on too thick' when I described the Nazis. 'People of a certain nationality dislike our foreign policy. That's quite understandable. *But they'd do best to keep their feelings to their family circle.*' This staggered me. I did not know yet what was in store for us."[157]

Ehrenburg personally discovered, that even though he voluntarily underwent the process of assimilation, there was no assurance that he would be accepted into Russian society. Young Jewish Communists were also baffled and disturbed. They had grown up in a socialist society, and knew no other. A Jewish test pilot, for instance, described his inner conflicts as follows:

> "… most of us accepted the treaty as one takes a dose of medicine: it was horrible but necessary. But the signing of the treaty was followed by happenings that were no longer understandable.

The fascists were no longer called fascists — it became impossible to find the word in the press and even in semi-official lectures and speeches. What we had been taught to abhor as hostile, evil and menacing from our Komsomol — nay, Pioneer — days, suddenly became, as it were neutral ... the feeling stole into our souls as we looked at photographs of Molotov standing next to Hitler, or read reports of Soviet grain and oil flowing into fascist Germany, or watched the Prussian goose-step being introduced at that very time into our armed forces. Yes, it was very difficult to understand what was what."[158]

All these problems, doubts and inner conflicts were suddenly forced into the background for the marriage of convenience, did not last very long. The Soviet peoples soon found themselves in a mortal struggle with Nazi Germany, early, on June 22, 1941. Germany attacked the Soviet Union, and German troops stormed across the western borders deep into the Ukraine and Belorussia. With the help of hindsight, it can be said that this factor changed the political development of the world, as well as the map of Europe for some time to come. Soviet Jews were no less affected by these developments, than the rest of the population.

Another marriage of convenience was quickly consummated. The "imperialist" enemies of Communism; namely, Britain and her allies, joined forces with the Soviet Union to fight the common enemy, Nazi Germany. Within Russia, controls on the Jews were partly relaxed as religion, in some aspects, experienced a revival. The war against Nazi Germany became the "Great Patriotic War," sometimes called the "Second War of the Fatherland."[159] It was a mortal struggle from the very first day. The Nazi armies advanced quickly and deeply into Soviet territory, and Stalin summoned all available internal forces for the defence of the fatherland. He appealed to Russian nationalism and patriotism, and invoked famous names in Russian history, such as Alexander Nevsky, who defeated the Teutonic Knights in the thirteenth century, and Alexander Suvorov and Michael Kutuzov, two Russian generals who fought against Napoleon.

The suspension of anti-religious propaganda benefited Soviet Jewry, because synagogues remained the only places where Jews could have assembled together, and were given the freedom to worship. The synagogues were overcrowded in the main cities, which included large Jewish populations. Prayers were offered for a speedy Soviet victory, and for the victims of Nazi aggression.[160] For the first time, there was no anti-religious propaganda campaign, during the Jewish High Holidays.[161] Synagogues were full of Jews of all age groups, except those in the army. The information about religious services was officially posted in many public places, an important change from previous restrictions. The Jews were urged to pray for the victory of the Red Army.[162] And when the defence of Moscow was secured, special thanksgiving prayers were offered at the great synagogue in Moscow, with many Jewish Red Army soldiers and Jewish recruits of the Polish army present.[163] This relaxation of controls on religious activities, was accompanied by a suspension of anti-religious propaganda in general. The Militant Atheist League discontinued the publication of its organ *Bezbozhnik*. The Associated Press (A.P.) was cited as reporting "that instructions have been issued for the entire suppression of the anti-religious campaign among Jews.[164]

The Soviet government was anxious to spread in the Allied and neutral countries the news of the official Soviet attitude towards religion. S.A. Lozovsky, Deputy Chief of the Sovinformburo, said in a press conference:

"... worship is free in the U.S.S.R.... Religion is a private affair for the Soviet citizens, in which the state does not interfere, and considers it unnecessary to interfere...."[165]

Lozovsky further added that the Soviet government had allocated special funds for the building of synagogues, and the repair of old ones.[166] The daily bulletin of the Soviet Embassy in London gave some interesting statistics about religious practices in the U.S.S.R. Listing various creeds and sects, it stated:

"... believers freely practice their religious worship, celebrate festivals, fasts, elect leaders of religious communities, etc. The Soviet Government provides buildings for religious purposes free of

charge and exempt of taxes, and ensures that no-one disturbs the
rights of believers, offends their feelings or jeers at their beliefs.
Infringement of the rights of believers is severely punished. The
clergy enjoy equal rights with other citizens.

The bulletin further added there were 1,011 synagogues and
2,559 Rabbis in the USSR."[167]

The use of Yiddish as the language of official communication
between the government and its Jewish subjects, seemed an obvious
indication of change in government policy towards Soviet Jewry. The
use of Yiddish in schools, courts, and research had been denied to Soviet
Jewry since the late thirties. The exceptions were the then recently
annexed or occupied territories of eastern Poland, the three Baltic States
and the two provinces of Rumania. In the annexed territories a process
of "Sovietization" was instituted, but it lasted only up to June 1941.[168]
The process provided for a more rapid development of "proletarian"
Yiddish and a quick adjustment to Soviet practices in the middle thirties. Therefore, when the Soviet government announced in July 1941,
special defence courses in Yiddish for the Jews in Leningrad, Kiev,
Kharkov, Odessa and many other cities, together with the marked concessions in religious freedoms, seemed to herald a change in policy that
was substantial indeed.[169] The first Soviet Jews to react publicly as an
"independent group," were some Yiddish writers and poets, who, in a
general appeal to Soviet Jews, stressed that "Hitler is not only an enemy
of progress and civilization, but also the arch enemy of the Jews."[170]

For the first of only two periods in recent political history, the interest of the Soviet peoples coincided with that of Soviet Jewry.[171] The
unusual combination of political and military developments, created a
situation in which Soviet Jews identified themselves fully and without
any reservations, with the interests of their fatherland and with the
unity of Jewish people around the world. This unity of interests gave
the Jewish leaders and Jewish intellectuals in the Soviet Union much
needed reassurance, confidence and inner security. This new turn in
history, enabled S. Mikhoels to later say: "I am the representative of *that
part* of the Jewish people, which lives in Soviet Russia."[172]

This unity of interests, provided the setting for an important meeting of Jewish intellectuals, writers, poets, artists and scientists, which was held in Moscow on August 24, 1941. This rally, the third to be held in 1941,[173] was called the "First Meeting of the Representatives of the Jewish People," and was reported in the Soviet Press. More importantly, it was broadcast in Yiddish over Moscow radio to the Jews of the world, who were addressed as "brider Yidn;" namely, our Jewish brethren.[174] It was the first time that the Soviet press was permitted to publish an appeal from Soviet Jews to the Jews outside their own country. The meeting and the appeal to world Jewry, was of great political significance, as an important milestone in Jewish national history. About twenty-five prominent Soviet Jewish personalities participated in the meeting. Ilya Ehrenburg, who was one of the participants, recalled the meeting in a short note on one of the other participants, the poet Peretz Markish. The passage indicates the underlying Soviet motivation for the meeting:

> "I remember a big meeting in Moscow in 1941; it was transmitted by radio to America. Peretz Markish, Sergei Eisenstein, S.M. Mikhoels, P.L. Kapitsa and I were the speakers. Markish appealed fervently to American Jews to call upon their country to join in the struggle against fascism *(America at that time being neutral)*."[175]

The meeting was a great event in the life of Soviet Jewry, and left a tremendous impact among the Jews of America and England. The *Jewish Chronicle* of London, in the midst of its centenary celebrations, gave the Moscow Jewish meeting prominent space on its front page. The following excerpt contains the gist of the Soviet appeal over the radio:

> "... Not one Jew throughout the whole world must be outside this struggle, said a Moscow radio broadcast, giving an account of a great Jewish meeting, when an appeal was made to the Jews of the world and especially to the Jews of Great Britain and the United States to give their utmost help in the war against Nazism. Jews in the occupied countries, were particularly called upon to do everything in their power to disrupt the economic resources

of the Fascists, to penetrate into their most vital branches of the
death-dealing industries and to paralyze them at all cost."[176]

Peretz Markisch, the Yiddish novelist and poet, said that "rivers and
seas are no barrier," and declared to his Jewish brothers that "*we are one
people, and now we are to be one army.*" David Bergelson, the writer, noted
that the Nazis were determined to obliterate the Jewish nation, but the
Jews, he added, were resolved to live and not to die. Sergei Eisenstein,
the film producer, called on Jews in all occupied countries to be equal
to their historic task.[177] The worldwide response to this appeal by
Soviet Jewry was heartening, as the Jewish press and Jewish organizations, irrespective of political differences, gave their full support. Even
Jews who had bitter personal experiences in Soviet jails, or who had
severely criticized the Soviet regime for the persecution of Zionists,
gave their full support. So did the orthodox Jews, whose anti-commu-
nist philosophy would have normally prevented any positive response
to Soviet appeals. The Jewish world seemed united, and this unity of
purpose became the theme of the day in London, New York, Jerusalem
and Moscow. Dr. Stephen Wise responded to the appeal on behalf of
the World Jewish Congress, as did Professor S. Brodetsky on behalf of
the British Board of Jewish Deputies, while the veteran leader of the
Palestinian Jews, M. Ussiskin, rose from his deathbed to convey a message of encouragement and support.[178]

S. Levenberg, veteran Zionist labor leader, responded in a leading
article in *Jewish Labor*, under the heading "The Soviet Union and the
Jewish Problem." He expressed the admiration of the Jewish people
throughout the world, for the courage and tenacity of men and women
of the Soviet Union, and stressed that "this common struggle has
brought Russian Jewry again, after 25 years of isolation, into closer contact with the Jewish peoples the world over."[179] The article concluded
with the hope that the Soviet Union will be able to "change those parts
of its Jewish policy, which have been unfavorable to the Jewish national
movement, Zionism. There is no logical reason," continued Levenberg,
"why there should be a conflict between World Jewry and the Soviet
Union; [and] why Russia should not be among the foremost supporters of the Jewish National Home in Palestine."[180]

The term "meeting of the representatives of the Jewish people" was used to increase the impact of the appeal. In a sense, Yiddish writers and poets, were representatives of the Jewish people, as writers of other nations consider themselves to be. But, strictly speaking, they were not elected representatives of either their professional organizations or some geographical constituency. However, there was no doubt that they had earned their status through hard work, so that by 1946, Ben Zion Goldberg could say:

"I told him [S.A. Lozovsky] that the committee seemed to be developing into a sort of Soviet Jewish Congress, and it might as well assume this function formally, even change its name accordingly, now that the war was over."[181]

Y.A. Gilboa, the Israeli writer, attached special "political" significance to this first public gathering of representatives of the Jewish people. "This gathering," wrote Gilboa, "may be regarded as having laid the ground for the establishment of the Jewish Anti-Fascist Committee."[182]

The assumption is supported by a statement of the first secretary of the J.A.C., Shakno Epstein, who also claimed that the J.A.C. was set up following the gathering of the representatives of the Jewish people, and that its activity began in February 1942.[183] It is seriously denied by others among them, Solomon M. Schwarz, who argued:

"A lengthy description of the meeting which took more than a full page in the next morning's Pravda, made no reference to plans for establishing any Jewish organization whatsoever. The gathering appealed to Jews throughout the world not to despair, not to await destruction passively, but to take an active part in the war against Hitlerite Germany. Not a single word was said about the establishment of a Jewish committee."[184]

Schwarz advanced the suggestion that the idea to form a political body that would speak for the Jewish people of Eastern Europe, was not of Soviet origin. He admitted that the J.A.C. was sponsored and directed by the [Soviet] government.[185] Salo W. Baron, has also supported the position taken by Schwarz.[186] B.Z. Goldberg, one of the writers, with the best access to Soviet sources and Soviet government officials, stated recently in a letter to this writer:

> "… I would have not noticed, nor would it seem reasonable to me, to connect Alter and Ehrlich [two Polish Bundist leaders] to the organization of the J.A.C. I would rather credit Lozovsky with the idea. He was head of Sovinformburo functioning on the international scene … the J.A.C. and the All-Slav Committee shared the same building. The two committees functioned on an international base, primarily in America."[187]

Therefore, the question of the origin of the J.A.C. remains controversial, at least until research can be resumed with full access to Soviet archives. I remain not entirely satisfied with either of the two views, supported as they are by circumstantial evidence now available.

The idea of such a committee may well have been conceived by the propaganda experts, with a view to repairing the Soviet image abroad, particularly among Jews in the United States. On the other hand, the United States was still neutral, and it would seem more likely that the Soviet government wished to reach American public opinion, through appeals to such large minority groups as the Jews and the Slavs in the United States. It was, therefore, not an accident that the J.A.C. was formed on the same day as four other committees, and that it shared the same building with the All-Slav Committee.

However, another development also took place and with the same idea in mind, but coming from the initiative of a different department. This was the Alter-Erlich project, which seemed to have been initiated by L.P. Beria, then Commissar of Internal Affairs, who was responsible for the internal security services. Was it a matter of pure coincidence that, in addition to plans prepared by the proper governmental agency (Sovinformburo), another set of plans was conceived by Beria's security services? What seems to be established so far is, first, that all committees were under the control of the information section of the Commissariat of Foreign Affairs, headed by A.S. Shcherbakov, one of the closest collaborators of

Stalin and a candidate-member of the Politburo.[188] Second, shortly after their release from prison, Erlich and Alter were visited by a colonel from Beria's security services, who suggested to the two Polish leaders, among other things, that "it was the view of the Soviet Government, that the Jews abroad, especially those in the neutral United States, could make a great contribution to the Soviet war effort. For this purpose, a Jewish World Committee should be formed, to be headed by Erlich and Alter."[189] Therefore, in both instances, the idea of the committee came from the Soviet authorities. Although, accounts differ in some details, it seems quite clear that both Erlich and Alter, agreed to cooperate with Beria, and after a full discussion with the latter and his officials, prepared a submission to the Soviet government on the matter. It seems, also, judging from a letter written by them to Beria, that he agreed with their design, and asked them to submit the plan in the form of a direct letter to Stalin.[190] The purpose of the direct submission to Stalin was "to request official authorization for the immediate establishment of a Jewish Anti-Hitlerite Committee" on the territory of the Soviet Union.[191]

All available evidence indicates that, in both projects, propaganda to the two Western countries; namely, England and the United States, was the main, if not the only reason for the Soviet interest in the establishment of a J.A.C. To briefly summarize, there were two views on the origin of the Committee. Those who claim that the idea was not of Soviet origin (Schwarz, Baron, Ainsztein), really assert that it originated with the two Polish-Jewish leaders, who were interested in creating an organization to primarily serve the interests of the Jewish people of Eastern Europe. Their plan called for many aims, which ran counter to known Soviet interests, including the active participation of Jewish communities outside the control of the Soviet Union, immediate help to Jewish refugees, and direct contact with Polish Jews through the channels of the Polish government in exile.[192] Other authors, including Goldberg, simply argue that the Jewish Anti-Fascist Committee was formed, because a need arose to have direct communication with Jewish communities in the Western and neutral countries. The Soviet government hoped that Jews could help in improving the Soviet image abroad, and at the same time, arouse anti-Nazi feelings. It remains a matter of speculation as to whether the Soviet government appraised the "power and importance" of Jews in the United States, as being so significant as to influence the decision of the U.S. government. In view of the fact that a Beria subordinate suggested such a committee to Erlich and Alter, and that the J.A.C. was formed within a general Soviet scheme under the control of Sovinformburo, it is difficult to accept the view that "the idea of a political body that would speak for the Jewish people of Eastern Europe was not of Soviet origin."[193] The Erlich and Alter project was not the only fact to obscure the origin of the J.A.C.'s formation. Just about the time that the two Bundist leaders were executed on December 4, 1941, Samuel Khobrutsky, President of the Moscow Jewish Community, announced from his temporary headquarters in Tashkent that "the Jewish affairs in the Soviet Union will be conducted from that city."[194] Is it possible that the Soviet decision-makers were undecided from the end of August 1941, when "the Moscow meeting of representatives of the Jewish people" laid the ground for the establishment of the Jewish Anti-Fascist Committee"[195] to April 23, 1942, when Lozovsky officially acknowledged its existence?[196]

Sources presently available for research on the events surrounding the origin of the J.A.C., are not considered sufficient to form a definitive answer. It is quite likely that it might never be possible to establish an undisputed cause-and-effect link between the Erlich and Alter project and the formation of the J.A.C., as we know it. It is, of course, more plausible to reject any such connection, as Goldberg and others did, if for no other reason than for the suggested terms of reference of the Anti-Hitlerite Committee, and for its personal composition. Certain doubts, however, remain, because it is not necessarily true that all Soviet policy decisions can be traced to logic, or must be consistent with known ideological precepts.

CHAPTER VI

THE STRUCTURE AND FUNCTION OF THE JEWISH ANTI-FASCIST COMMITTEE

When Lozovsky announced the formation of the J.A.C., he failed to provide for the publication of a constitution, which would explicitly outline the purpose of the Committee, its organizational structure and forms of membership. It was therefore necessary to study a wide variety of existing sources such as works, articles and unpublished manuscripts, to obtain some knowledge of these vital details of the Committee. When these sources did not produce results fully satisfactory to me, I wrote to individual authors, who could provide certain specific knowledge as to the organization of the J.A.C. However, such correspondence did not always bring precise answers. For example, one author, questioned on the selection of membership, wrote: "As to membership of the Executive Committee, it may have been selected by Epstein, Fefer or Mikhoels, and then received approval from the higher ups."[197] It therefore became necessary to supplement these gaps in the information by visiting the offices of certain organizations in New York, interview executive personnel, who were known for some aspects of their work with the J.A.C., and accomplish some research in the archives in Jerusalem. While certain aspects of the organizational framework remain a mystery, an attempt will be made in this chapter to give an outline of the structure and function of the J.A.C.

Let us briefly recapitulate what has been said in the concluding paragraphs of chapter five on the J.A.C. This organization was a Soviet-sponsored institution, created during the war as one of five committees charged with specific duties and aimed at particular sections of the population in various Allied and neutral countries. The other committees were: The All-Slav Committee, the Anti-Fascist Committee of Soviet Women, the Anti-Fascist Committee of Soviet Youth and the Anti-Fascist Committee of Soviet Scientists.[198] All five committees were formally under the exclusive direction and supervision of a special Soviet agency, the Sovinforburo. The agency was headed by A.S. Shcherbakov, but was actually run by S.A. Lozovsky, of whom Ehrenburg wrote, "He had no power — at every step he had to refer to Molotov or Shcherbakov."[199] The man responsible for the activities of the J.A.C. to the C.P.S.U. was S. Bregman, member of the Party Control Commission. He was present at most of the meetings, but hardly ever participated in its discussions.[200]

The top organ of the J.A.C. was *The Presidium*, whose members were chosen and appointed by the Party. The first Presidium consisted of S.M. Mikhoels, the actor and director of the Jewish Theatre in Moscow, who was named chairman; the Ukrainian Yiddish poet, Itsik Fefer, as vice-chairman; and Shakno Epstein, a journalist, and an old Party hand with a history of service in Beria's security force, as secretary. Upon Epstein's death, Fefer took over the position of secretary.[201] The authority of the state was represented by Lozovsky, and any major problems arising from the functions of the J.A.C. were referred to him. He was consulted by the J.A.C. leaders on the most sensitive issues, and undoubtedly served as a watch-dog over their actions.[202] This description of Lozovsky does not conflict with Ehrenburg's opinion that he had no power. Ehrenburg referred to important state decisions, such as the possible implications of his report on German statements in occupied France, about the German plans to attack the Soviet Union. Redlich, on the other hand, described day-to-day problems, arising in the organization and function of the J.A.C.

The Executive Committee consisted of two types of members. The first were the Yiddish writers and poets, such as Peretz Markish, David Bergelson, David Hofstein, Samuel Halkin and others. "They rightly regarded themselves as the spiritual leaders of the Soviet Jewish community, and as the creative artists of an international literature with leaders and followers where Yiddish was spoken."[203] The second were people who were asked by the Party to lend their prestige and authority to the J.A.C., but seldom participated in its daily activities. Some of them had a Jewish background or were otherwise interested in Jewish life, while others were not. In this category, were the Party journalist David Zaslavsky; General Jacob Kreizer; General Aaron Katz, head of the faculty for motorized forces at the Stalin Military Academy [204]; film producer Sergei Eisenstein; physicist C.P. Kapitsa; scientist Lena Shtern. There was also Ilya Ehrenburg, who did not speak Yiddish and wished to remain outside of Jewish society, even though he had previously participated in the work of the J.A.C. He attended the work sessions of the plenary meetings, and gave the most lively and dramatic descriptions of Jewish suffering and Jewish heroism. He was particularly concerned with counteracting the German propaganda, which described Jews as avoiding military service, as cowards and as poor soldiers. During his active period, he was at times critical of the J.A.C.,[205] in the sense that it was not doing enough. The exact number of the members of the Executive Committee in 1942 is not known.

The majority of people associated with the work of the J.A.C., were writers and poets and "with a poet as secretary and an intellectual actor as president."[206] "The Association of Jewish Writers was an autonomous body, connected only with the Union of Soviet Writers."[207] The J.A.C. had no local groups in the country and no "connection with any other organized Jewish group in the Soviet Union,"[208] be it the Yiddish theaters, or publishing houses, synagogues, etc.

This formal isolation of the J.A.C. from other Jewish institutions, was consistent with the Party policy and also with the inclusion of the J.A.C., as one of the five committees in the Sovinformburo. The object was to keep it functionally separated from activities *within* the Soviet Union, something which proved difficult, if not impossible to accomplish. Writing of the avowed purpose of the J.A.C., Goldberg commented that one reason which led Mikhoels and Fefer *to disregard it* was the fact that " ... so strong was the current of Jewish life in the Soviet Union, so urgent the need for a central Jewish body, that the *greater part of the activity was, in actuality*, concerned with local Jewish matters."[209] The transformation of intent and purpose, which seemingly forced itself upon the leaders of the J.A.C., may have been a strong contributory factor to the reasons for its demise in 1948.

The next organ of the J.A.C. was the Plenum, whose main activities were divided into public meetings of "representatives of the Jewish people,"[210] and plenary sessions. The Plenum convened annually, the first being in May 1942, the second in February 1943, and the third in April

1944. The first of these public meetings (that is, disregarding the August 1941 meeting held before the actual formation of the J.A.C.), appealed to Soviet and non-Soviet Jews to take up arms and fight the common enemy. The secretary of the committee, Shakno Epstein, emphasized that "the destiny of all freedom loving peoples, depended on the outcome of the battle in the Soviet Union," and that "the Jewish people must clearly realize that they cannot exist in peace, as long as Fascism exists."[211] At each of the plenary sessions a special appeal to the Jews of the world was drafted and approved. The appeal of the first plenary session warned the Jews of America and Great Britain that "there must not be a minute's delay in dealing the death blow to Hitler's armies," and urged speed, because "we are on the eve of the summer of 1942, which is destined to decide the fate of mankind, and the fate of the Jewish people."[212]

Among the new names added to the list of speakers were Ilya Spivak, corresponding member of the Ukrainian Academy of Sciences and director of its Jewish cultural section; A. Strongin, manager of the Der Emes Publishing House; Alexander Frumkin, member of the Academy of Sciences; Grigory Tsitrinovich, an army physician; and Colonel Feivel Michlin. The military theme ran through most of the speeches and was indicative of the situation and the needs of Soviet defence. A special appeal was made to Jewish officers and men of the Red Army to volunteer for demanding and specialized duties. They were called upon to volunteer for service as snipers, pilots, tank commanders, and were urged to join the elite military detachments, the so-called "guard regiments."[213] Jews in the Nazi occupied countries were urged to join the partizans. All the public meetings and appeals to world Jewry were broadcast from Moscow.

The plenary session which followed covered matters related to the basic activities of the J.A.C. The decision was made to divide the plenum into four subcommittees, each with a specific project. A committee was set up to collect material on the participation of Soviet Jews in the war. This committee later supplied material for the publication of the *Black Book* in 1946. It also provided material for irregularly published news releases about the number of Jews decorated in the war, their relative strength in the armed forces, and so on. The next committee planned to collect information on Nazi atrocities against Soviet Jews. They also formed two permanent committees, one for J.A.C. publications and the other dealing with financial matters.

On the eve of the first anniversary of the German attack on the Soviet Union, it was decided to make a worldwide appeal for moral and financial support. In it, the Soviet Union was called "the first force in the war against Hitlerism, and Soviet Jews were praised for the example they set the Jewish people."[214] The particular part of the appeal which referred to funds read: "Jews throughout the world! Let us collect money, buy a thousand tanks and five hundred airplanes, and ship them to the Red Army!"[215] Throughout the next months, appeals for funds were reported from Baku,[216] Tashkent and Ufa.[217] Yiddish writers read from their works, and General Jacob Kreizer, member of the executive committee of the J.A.C., spoke on behalf of Soviet Jewish soldiers.[218] In the United States, a Jewish Division of American War Relief was organized, in Britain a Jewish Fund for Soviet Russia, and in Uruguay a Jewish Committee for Aid to Russia. All these divisions and committees were formed for the purpose of aiding the Soviet Union. Particular mention should be made of the direct response to the fundraising appeal given by such groups as the Victory League of Palestine,[219] and the Jewish Trade Unionists (a group of about two hundred members of the AFO-CIO), the latter appealing to American Jews "to provide one thousand tanks and five hundred bombers for the Soviet forces."[220]

No reference was found in any of the issues of *Aynikayt* published between June 1942 and December 1944, or in the daily bulletins, of the *J.T.A. (Jewish Telegraphic Agency)* about the purchasing of any tanks or planes, or the use of the collected monies for any similar purposes. There was no reference found to a presentation of a tank or plane, named after one of the biblical heroes (such as Bar Kochba) or writers, such as Judah Halevy, Heinrich Heine or Sholom Alechem. No accounting was ever published, as to how the monies collected, either in the Soviet Union or abroad, were spent.[221]

Between the first meeting of "Jewish representatives" in August 1941, and the second in May 1942, twenty-two other prominent persons joined the ranks of the committee to appeal to world Jewry. Most of the new participants came from among the military forces, professionals, chairmen of collectives, and some Party and state officials from Birobidzhan.

There is more information about the second plenary session, which was held from the 18th to the 20th of February, 1943.[222] Most of the speakers were reported, in the official organ *Aynikayt*. In spite of this editing, the speeches disclosed two trends: the first strictly followed the party line, which narrowly delimited the scope and the functions of the committee as laid down by Moscow, and the second, which went beyond Party directives because some participants expressed the needs of Soviet Jewry as they saw them from close observation. The second plenary meeting consisted of four working sessions with delegates[223] from various parts of the country. Among them were ten writers, seven poets, and two artists, the balance consisting of army personnel, directors of enterprises, professional men and chairmen of collective farms. A total of twenty-eight speakers participated in the debates, as recorded in a special issue of *Aynikayt,* devoted to the Second Plenary Meeting.[224]

Just as the military theme was the character of the first plenary meeting, the second was also important, as it dealt with attempts to define the role or function of the J.A.C. Chairman Mikhoels, began his opening speech with a review of the past ten months and described the achievements of the Red Army on all fronts. He estimated the loss of Jewish lives, up to March 1943, at four million, and praised all those who actively participated in the war against Hitler. Of the twenty-eight speakers, twenty wished to enlarge the scope of activities of the J.A.C. Some criticized the distribution of the paper *Aynikayt* ("it cannot be seen anywhere in Moscow"). Others were unhappy with its content, and recommended that it should devote space to Jewish human interest stories from Soviet cities. The boldest criticism came from those who wished to rebuild the J.A.C. into an organ of Soviet Jewry. The following examples indicate the mood of the speakers and the issues of the day, as they saw them. The poet David Hofstein, spoke of his concern for the welfare of the surviving Jews, and called for immediate action by the J.A.C.:

"The J.A.C. did much, but we must concern ourselves with what we shall find in the cities liberated by the Red Army. When we return back, what shall we find? Nothing, but destruction and graves. We must prepare for re-construction. Let us worry about the living people, and let us worry in time."[225]

Abraham Kahan, a writer, wished to enlarge the function of the J.A.C. He suggested that the J.A.C. appoint local reporters in all cities with a large Jewish population, and recommended improvements for a better distribution of *Aynikayt*. Continued Kahan, "Since the destruction of the great libraries in Kiev, Kharkov and in other cities, efforts must be made to collect the scattered remnants of our cultural heritage."[226] Writer, Noah Lurie, advocated that a liaison be established between Jewish writers and Red Army front line units, so that "their reports should describe the smell of fresh wounds." He suggested that writers could perform a useful function by seeing for themselves what life was like for those who escaped the enemy and survived unspeakable hardships. Records should be kept not only for the sake of historical truth, but also for the sake of justice when the day of reckoning came for those who perpetrated genocide. David Wolkenstein expressed the view that "the most important aspect of the work of the J.A.C. is that a forum was established for the best individuals among our people," such as writers, poets and artists. Their work was well known all over Europe, America and indeed the world, therefore, making it possible for mankind to know the truth about the situation. Professor Y. Nusinov reminded the meeting not to dwell in the past, but to speak about what has to be accomplished in the future. It was true that their main efforts should be aimed at worldwide publicity of the problem. He then added, "we should not limit ourselves to propaganda." The committee should also concern itself with the work inside the country, and should provide help to evacuated people. Furthermore, the paper *Aynikayt* should mirror the life of Soviet Jewish masses in the hinterland. Writer S. Parsov, recommended a more systematic collection of historical evidence. All the known facts of the participation of Jewish masses in the War of the Fatherland should be recorded.

The secretary of the J.A.C., Shakno Epstein, attempted to lead the discussions away from tasks "that would burden the J.A.C. and have nothing to do with the fight against Fascism,"[227] — an obvious reference to all those who recommended new functions for the J.A.C. In his summary of the J.A.C.'s activities during the past year, Epstein reported the committee had established contacts with one hundred correspondents all over the Soviet Union, and with various Jewish organizations abroad. More than five thousand letters were received from Soviet Jews, and in the same period, eight thousand pages of printed material were sent abroad.[228]

Chairman Mikhoels, answered some of the critics, but summed up the main issued in a way which indicated clearly that he was leaning "toward a broader interpretation of the Committee's functions."[229] As he explained:

> "They [the speakers] had one single aim, namely to strengthen our work. The discussions showed particularly the concern about the function and scope of the activities of the Committee. There were some who have forgotten that this Committee is a fighting organization, and has one clear and definite task to consolidate all the forces in the struggle against Fascism.
>
> Yet, there is some desgree of truth in the remarks made, that the Committee has not yet become for the Jewish population in our land that living center it ought to have been. People write letters about their painful problems from various places; the scattered Jewish population is searching for an address, and we are not allowed to disregard it.
>
> We ought to show initiative. We have to address this and other questions to the proper authorities. It was quite properly pointed out that our activities entered a new phase.
>
> … Today the time has arrived to talk with a different tone. We have the right to demand, and the right to accuse those (among Jews) who don't do their duty. We feel that the Jewish people gave us authority to do that."[230]

Considering the cautionary language used by all speakers of the meeting to express the prevailing mood, it is not difficult to agree with Mikhoels's conclusions, particularly when he described what seemed to be a general consensus that "the scattered Jewish population is searching for an address, and we are not allowed to disregard it."

The tone of his concluding words indicated clearly the change, which took place within the J.A.C., and the intention to pay full attention to the "will of the Jewish population." Within a short space of time, Soviet Jewry seemed to have acquired a new image, and perhaps its leaders were right in claiming, in the words of Mikhoels, that "... the Jewish people gave us the right to demand authority within Soviet Jewry," and the responsibility to "show initiative" toward the Soviet government. These words indicate an attempt to transform the J.A.C. from "a propaganda weapon of the Soviet department of information"[231] into a very active Jewish national organization.

Some authors go beyond this interpretation of the development within the J.A.C. and argue against Schwarz and West, both of whom held the view that the J.A.C. was of small significance to the Jewish people. Schwarz, commenting on the summary suppression of the J.A.C. in the fall of 1948, wrote that, "It was scarcely a loss to the Jewish population of Russia."[232] However, the Israeli author Szmeruk, known for his essays on the literary value of Yiddish publications in the Soviet Union, wrote critically of the appraisals of the J.A.C. made by Schwarz and West. Szmeruk asserted that "neither of them differentiate between the sincere efforts and great desire of many of the Committee's leaders to set up an internal representative body, and obstacles placed in their way by the Soviet authorities."[233] Knowing the nature of these obstacles, it was indeed surprising that so much was attempted within five years after the purges eliminated not only the last of the Jewish literary elite, but suppressed Yiddish newspapers and periodicals, and also closed down all remaining Jewish cultural institutions.

Between the second and third plenary sessions, an official Soviet Jewish mission, the only one of its kind, was appointed to travel abroad in the "interest of Soviet Jewry." The importance of the visit, from a Jewish point of view, cannot be overestimated. After a separation of over a quarter of a century, Soviet Jewry rejoined the mainstream of Jewish life. "Theirs was definitely a Jewish mission,"[234] wrote one author, "for they came exclusively to organized Jewry and addressed the public only in Yiddish. And it was the Kremlin that sent them on this mission."[235] The mission was indeed rare as a form of cultural exchange. There was no other mission of this kind arranged or permitted for any of the other minority nationalities of the U.S.S.R. It still remains a mystery why this type of mission was authorized by the Soviet officials, and any explanation for the reasons behind its purpose remains speculative. Officially, the mission was approved by the Soviet government in response to a "joint invitation of the American Committee of Jewish Writers, Artists and Scientists and the Jewish Division of American Russian War Relief."[236] In fact, the suggestion to invite such a mission came from a "prominent American Communist"[237] who reported that the J.A.C. "wished to send a delegation to the United States."[238] Therefore, the initiative was Moscow's, and the personnel of the mission was also chosen exclusively by the Soviet government. When the composition of the mission, consisting of Mikhoels and Fefer, was reported at a meeting of the Executive Committee of the Jewish Division of the American Russian War Relief, Shalom Ash, the well-known Jewish novelist, objected to the inclusion of Fefer. He suggested the inclusion of David Bergelson, a much better known Soviet Yiddish writer, but the American Communist insisted Fefer must be invited...."[239]

In addition to being an official Soviet mission, it was known that before leaving the Soviet Union, Mikhoels and Fefer took leave of President Kalinin in his office and "Stalin himself came in by a side door to pat the prodigals on the back and wish them success."[240] Therefore, the mission had the personal blessing of Stalin himself, a fact which indicates that the dictator considered the undertaking important. But exactly what the interests of the Soviet Union were remains a matter of speculation. Moreover, the members of the mission while speaking to mass meetings of American Jews, threw no light on the question. They addressed themselves to their Jewish audiences as if there never was a quarter of a century of forced isolation between them; for example, Fefer stated to a mass rally of 47,000 New York Jews that:

"The Jews in the Soviet Union and in the United States are the majority of the Jewish People. Together we are ten million Jews. Upon us lies the responsibility for the fate of the Jewish people."[241]

From an isolation, which was so complete in the case of Soviet Jewry, to a sudden political claim of responsibility or the "fate of the Jewish people," is a significant reversal of policy — welcome no doubt from a Jewish point of view — but hard to comprehend in terms of Soviet political realities. Leaving speculation aside, Fefer's statement was a clear indication of an intent to establish closer ties between the Soviet Jewry and world Jewry, and the recognition of the need for a single Jewish centre to provide much needed political leadership. It was one of the most important statements made by the two members of the mission, because it remained consistent with the trend of many other statements which followed.

One of the results of this visit was a new awareness of unity within the Jewish people, and the leaders of the American and British Jewries began to think and to speak in practical terms of the necessity of having Soviet Jews formally associated within the organizational framework of world Jewry. It was at this time that during a visit of Mikhoels and Fefer to London, the delegates of the Workmen's Circle at the National Conference of the British Section of the World Jewish Congress, submitted a resolution inviting Soviet Jewry to join the World Jewish Congress. The resolution was enthusiastically acclaimed and approved by the Conference.[242] Speaking to a press conference shortly afterwards, Milkhoels forecasted "an end to the isolation of Soviet Jewry from World Jewry, after the war."[243] Fefer, spoke at the same Conference about the development of Jewish culture on the Soviet Union, and expressed hope "that it would be further stimulated after the war through contact with the Jews of other lands."[244] It was here that the stage was set for the negotiations to affiliate Soviet Jews to the World Jewish Congress. The negotiations took place a year later, in the winter of 1944, in Moscow.

Upon their return from a successful trip, Mikhoels and Fefer began preparations for one of the most impressive meetings to take place in wartime Moscow. Before an audience of over two thousand Moscow Jews, the opening session of the Third Plenum of the Representatives of the Jewish People and of the J.A.C. was held on April 2, 1944, in the Hall of Columns of the Soviet Trade Unions Building.[245] Fifty greetings were read from representative Jewish bodies, from a dozen countries. Among them were cables from the World Jewish Congress, signed by Rabbi S.S. Wise and Dr. Nahum Goldman; from the international orthodox religious organization Aqudas Israel, signed by Rabbi Jacob Rosenheim; and from the National Jewish Council in Palestine, signed by Ben-Zvi. "In long speeches aglow with pride of achievement, Mikhoels and Fefer gave all details of their triumphant tour," noted Goldberg in his description of the occasion. The speakers concluded with a "declaration that they had forged a world anti-Fascist Jewish unity."[246]

It was an event Moscow Jews were not to forget. The message of unity of the Jewish people was brought back to the Soviet Union by the same Soviet mission, whose members asserted it repeatedly in hundreds of meetings across the United States, Mexico, Canada and Great Britain. Now the message was being proclaimed inside the U.S.S.R., and Goldberg noted "the delegates [to the Third Plenum] were enthusiastic about the report. Mikhoels and Fefer, served their fatherland well, and had also broken the long isolation from the brethren abroad."[247] The meeting was also indicative of the prevailing mood in the Soviet Union about the outcome of the war. Optimism was replaced by assurance that victory was at hand.

About fifteen speakers addressed the audience,[248] among them the Submarine Commander Captain Goldberg, who recalled the exploits of Jewish fleet air-arm pilots in battle, Lieut. Col. Milner, Hero of the Soviet Union, and Lev Gonor, director of a munitions plant and a Hero of Socialist Labor. As Mikhoels stated with pride, "Jews hold fourth place, among 113 nationalities fighting in the ranks of the Red Army, who had been decorated."[249] Lina Shtern, a member of the Soviet Academy of Sciences, who only a few days previously was awarded the Order of the Red Banner of Labor said that, "by 1944, over 32,000 Jewish soldiers of the Red Army had been decorated for gallantry, and more than a hundred Jews received the title Hero of the Soviet Union."[250] Secretary Epstein, joined the prevailing mood of the meeting by a detailed account of the number of Jews among the decorated soldiers of the lied Army. He also stressed that there was a high percentage of Soviet Yiddish writers who had died in battle.[251] As in the opening public evening, so too were the working sessions of the Third Plenum dominated by the new element; namely, the soldiers of various branches of the armed forces. They replaced, to a degree, the dominating position previously held by writers, poets and artists in the J.A.C.

"The Second Plenum as opposed to the Third, was primarily concerned with enlarging the operative scope of the J.A.C., and the composition of the participants in the two plenary meetings mirrored this intention. The increased numbers among the participants were in direct relation to the increased role the J.A.C. began to play in the life of Soviet Jewry. It should, therefore, come as no surprise that the authority on Jewish literature in the U.S.S.R., Ch. Szmeruk, wrote in his summary:

> "The Jewish Anti-Fascist Committee, not only became the centre of all Jewish communal activity in U.S.S.R. and well known to the Jews of U.S.S.R. and World Jewry, but also became a centre of Jewish literature unparalleled in the history of Jews of U.S.S.R."[252]

Szmeruk was not alone in this evaluation of the position of the J.A.C. No less an expert on Soviet Jewry, Goldberg commented that the officers of the J.A.C. were fully aware that they had extended their terms of reference beyond the approved limits. However, commented Goldberg:

> "... so strong was the current of Jewish life in the Soviet Union, so urgent the need for a *central Jewish body*, that the greater part of the activity of the committee was, in actuality, concerned with *local Jewish matters*."[253]

The overall extension of the activities of the J.A.C. continued in the summer and fall of 1944. To many, it was now evident that the final defeat of Fascist militarism was not far away. Preparations were made in the Soviet Union (and in the two capitals of the two main Western allies, London and Washington) for postwar political settlements. Similar to Jewish organizations in the West, Soviet Jews within the J.A.C. busied themselves with collecting testimonies on Nazi atrocities from survivors, and increasing their wide contacts with Jewish organizations abroad. Much importance was attached to the documentation of the material collected by the now substantially enlarged staff of writers, researchers, specialists and secretaries. The subcommittee created at the First Plenum, in May 1942, was now a permanent part of the organizational structure. Ehrenburg and the writer, Vassily Grossman, edited much of the material collected for the Yiddish edition of the *Black Book*.[254] Material collected abroad was regularly mailed to the J.A.C., and the contacts between similar offices abroad and the J.A.C., were increasingly extended. As a result of all this expansion in its activities, coupled no doubt by the Party's determination to assure tighter control over these expanding functions, a number of structural changes within the organization were effected. It is not clear whether these changes originated within the J.A.C. or with the Party, but they were reported in the Committee's official organ, *Aynikayt*.[255] Seventeen new members were added to the J.A.C. during the third plenary working session. Among them were the poet Abraham Sutskever, the writer Vassily Grossman and others, including several high-ranking officers of the Red Army. The presidium was enlarged to fifteen members. The largest group by occupation remained were writers and poets, some of whom had established international reputations. Some among the less active members who were originally asked by the Party to join the J.A.C., so as to enhance its prestige, were now added to the presidium. This number included Lina Shtern, Dr. B. Shimelovich and General Jacob Kreizer. The presidium was again enlarged in August 1944, by four high-ranking Soviet officials, making a total of nineteen members. They were: S. Bregman, Deputy Minister of State Control of the U.S.S.R., Gubelman and Z. Bricker, two trade union officials, and L. Scheinin, Director of Engineering Courses in the Ministry of Railroad Transportation.[256]

These changes in membership and organizational structure may have contributed to a more balanced composition between the activist writers and poets (called "emotional and nationalistic" in a report by

Secretary Shakno Epstein), and the Party's appointed technocrats and apparatchiki. However, at this time, it in no way affected the connections of the J.A.C. with world Jewry, and it also did not influence the open channels of communication between the J.A.C. and the World Jewish Congress. In fact, communication between these two organizations, substantially increased during this very period. This extensive description and analysis of the Plenum was considered appropriate, because its work was visible through the edited versions of the minutes as they appeared in the issues of the *Aynikayt*. It also remained the only forum in which the participating members expressed their views on issues particularly relevant to the domestic problems of Soviet Jewry.

The subcommittees within the J.A.C. were either on-going structures, created to deal with day-to-day important business, (for example, financial affairs) or *ad hoc* bodies devised for special projects or emergency situations, which might arise from time to time. Among the first and more important subcommittees, was the one dealing with the *Black Book* project. The *Black Book* was to have been a documentary, compiled from material collected mostly by the J.A.C. from letters, testimonies, eye witness accounts and diaries. It was to be edited in Moscow and in New York, and when published, it would carry the imprint of three cities (New York, Moscow and Jerusalem), representing three important Jewish communities in the world at that time. The publication was to have been sponsored jointly by two special committees, one in New York and the other in Moscow.

The Moscow committee consisted of General Katz, S. Bregman, of the Party Control Committee, L. Honor, the director of munitions, Vassily Grossman, Lina Shtern, and Ilya Ehrenburg. According to Goldberg, the New York committee consisted of representatives of the World Jewish Congress and the American Committee of Jewish Writers, Artists and Scientists. However, the World Jewish Congress representative objected to the inclusion of Goldberg's committee "on the ground that unlike the other three organizations (the World Jewish Congress, the J.A.C., and Vaad Leumi), it was not a body representing Jewish communities."[257] In the end, the J.A.C. insisted on the inclusion of the American Committee of Jewish Writers, Artists and Scientists as "an absolute condition" of cooperation, and the World Jewish Congress

reluctantly yielded on this point. Therefore, the beginning of the cooperation between the two organizations was not too suspicious,[258] and
differences increased as the association continued. First, M.L.
Perlzweig,[259] maintained he never saw the final draft of the *Black Book,*
before it was published. When he finally saw the published version, he
took "the strongest exception to what had been produced because it
not only suffered from serious technical defects, but there were pas-
sages, which were heavily slanted from an ideological point of view."[260]
Also, a Yiddish edition was to have been published in Moscow, but the
project was abandoned. There was no mention of this fact in *Aynikayt,*
and no reason was given for the failure to produce the book. Goldberg
believed that "a power above Mikhoels and Fefer, who entered the
commitment in good faith, was responsible for the default, having from
the first meant the book for consumption abroad only."[261]

The composition of the Black Book Committee in New York bore
some resemblances to the first "coalition governments," established in
East European capitals after the war. Approximately, a fifty-fifty division
was maintained between the pro-Soviet and national Jewish elements.
The pro-Soviet half of the Committee made all the decisions, therefore
creating a rift of a permanent nature in the Committee's deliberations.
In the dispute surrounding the publication of the *Black Book,* Dr.
Perlzweig's objections were without effect, because they were made
much too late. He defended the lack of public repudiation by expressing fear that "a controversy might have proven very damaging to the
diplomatic situation at the time."[262]

In view of the Soviet government's expressed policy in favour of par-
tition of Palestine, the representatives of the World Jewish Congress
understandably played down their association with the Black Book
project. Therefore, when a copy of the *Black Book* was presented to the
mayor of New York at a mass meeting of some 15,000 people in
Madison Square Garden, the front page, listing the organizations responsible for the publication, was removed at Perlzweig's insistence.[263]
Another problem within the Black Book Committee, related to a wide
spread appeal for funds in the United States and Canada. The appeal was
promoted on behalf of the American Committee of Jewish Writers,

Artists and Scientists, but the propaganda material used implied it acted on behalf of the World Jewish Congress, the Vaad Leumi and the J.A.C. Objections were raised by the World Jewish Congress and the Canadian Jewish Congress, and an agreement was secured to effect the submission of periodical financial accounts to the World Jewish Congress. However, there is no evidence that this was ever done.[264]

On a whole, the cooperation within the Black Book Committee in New York was sadly lacking. It was also a bad beginning for what was planned to be a much larger "joint" publication program for the postwar period. There was to be a book about Jewish heroes in the Second World War, and a special committee was established in Moscow to plan and edit such a book. It consisted of such important Jewish public figures as the writer Vassily Grossman, General Katz and S. Bregman, whose participation in each of the aforementioned committees would indicate the interest of the Party. The publication was to be called *Jewish Heroes in the Struggle Against Fascism*. The Moscow committee was given the responsibility to provide the relevant manuscripts for the East, while the New York committee of the *Black Book* was given the task for the West. The book was to have appeared in Russian, Yiddish and English. Another project was to have been a Yiddish literary quarterly, [265] but none of these projects materialized. The Moscow committee proceeded with the prepatory work for the book on Jewish heroes, but it too was never published. Before it reached the printer, the Communist gauntlet fell on all the committee's activities.[266] Perlzweig summarized his experiences within the New York committee as follows:

"I was assigned the rather difficult task of cooperating with the representatives of the J.A.C. in the publication of the *Black Book*. It was not only a disappointing experience, it was devastating." "… so far as I can recall, we have since made no public reference to our participation in it."[267]

A study of documents published by the World Jewish Congress since the end of the Second World War, revealed no reference to the *Black Book*. Both Dr. N. Goldman's autobiography and the official history of the World Jewish Congress, fail to make any references to the project.[268] This was not accidental. One of the officials of the World Jewish Congress (Dr. Oscar Karbach), who took part in the compilation of the history, admitted "these omissions were deliberate."[269]

An interesting postscript on the *Black Book* project was offered by Ilya Ehrenburg, in an interview with an American journalist. Ehrenburg spoke of the murder of Mikhoels: "I was the first to state openly that he was murdered," and then spoke of the arrest of a large number of Jewish writers, and the beginning of the process of wiping out the record of Jewish martyrdom and heroism in World War II. The journalist then continued:

> "Ehrenburg told me the story of the suppression of the *Black Book*, a collection of documents and accounts of Nazi massacres and Jewish resistance, which was edited by himself and Vassily Grossman."
>
> "When they disbanded the Jewish Anti-Fascist Committee, they destroyed the type for the book, as well as the first sheets of the press. Luckily, I saved many of the original documents, and now the *Black Book* is again being prepared for publication."[270]

Whether Ehrenburg himself made arrangements for the publication is not really known. However, the *Black Book* has never been published in the Soviet Union.

Although, not attached to the J.A.C., several institutions were also engaged in Yiddish cultural activities in the U.S.S.R., during the same period that J.A.C. flourished. These were the Association of Jewish Writers, a section of the Union of Soviet Writers, the Yiddish State Theater, the Jewish "cabinet" in Kiev and Der Emes publishing house. The Yiddish State Theatre, one of the two major Yiddish cultural institutions in the Soviet Union during the Second World War, was a huge enterprise occupying its own three buildings and running on a budget of three million rubles a year. It employed three hundred persons, among them sixty actors.[271] The theater had a Yiddish dramatic school with about sixty students and a curriculum drafted by its director S.

Mikhoels. The Emes publishing house was a similarly large enterprise, and it was completely reorganized in 1943, through the efforts of the J.A.C.[272] As all Soviet enterprises, it had its own five-year plan, and, for example, in 1946 the list of planned publications contained 150 new titles, among them "several major undertakings, such as a comprehensive history of Yiddish literature, to mark the four-hundredth anniversary of Eliahu Bakhur."[273]

Seventy-nine titles were published by Emes during the war, as shown by the following statistical breakdown:

TABLE I
Soviet Books and Pamphlets in Yiddish, after June 22, 1941, to the End of the War.[274]

Years	1941	1942	1943	1944	1945	Total
Titles	21	2	24	18	14	79

Though none of these four institutions became organic parts of the organizational structure of the J.A.C., nevertheless, they were connected through many professional and personal ties. None of their directors would have "moved a step without consulting with the officers of the [J.A.C.] committee in Moscow. All of them were only too happy to put themselves under the spreading wings of the committee."[275] This was certainly an indication that the J.A.C. was perceived as not only the spiritual centre of the Jewish community in the Soviet Union, but also as its protector and leader. Therefore, it was a common belief "that its officers were close to the Kremlin and would guide it through the uncertainties of the postwar period."[276]

The *Aynkayt* was the official organ of the J.A.C. and one of its three medias of communication. The other two were radio broadcasts and special mailed news-sheets to news agencies, Jewish papers and organizations abroad. The first issue of *Aynikayt* appeared in Kuibyshev on June 7, 1942, and at first the paper was published every ten days. Late in July 1943, the editorial board moved to Moscow, and the paper became a weekly. From February 1945, the *Aynikayt* was published three times a week, an indication of the growing demand for a Yiddish newspaper. The editor was Shakno Epstein, and upon his death on July 21, 1945, G. Zhitz became its acting editor. The members of the editorial board at the time were D. Bergelson, Y. Dobrushin, Sh. Halkin, S. Mikhoels, L. Strongin, I. Fefer, L. Kvitko and A. Kushmirov.[277]

The Jewish reading public wrote hundreds of letters to the editor of the paper, expressing satisfaction with the publication, and small notes began to appear in *Aynikayt*, starting with the issue of July 7, 1942. In these notes, brief extracts from the letters were printed. The letter writers were mostly soldiers arid partizans, who described how the paper was passed from hand to hand at the frontlines of battle.[278] The *Aynikayt* at first had a column under the heading "Jewish News," which was later changed to "Around the World." This column contained information concerning Jews outside the Soviet Union, or as much of it as space and censorship permitted. However, most of the news recorded in the column was related to support given to the Soviet war effort.

There were two additional cultural activities in which the J.A.C. was active, both within the domestic field. The promotion of publication of Yiddish books began shortly after the first plenary session in May 1942. The J.A.C. informed seventy writers that it would undertake the publication of their works. For the next six months, details of the program were discussed with a special department, dealing with literary works. Broad topics, such as defence, the struggle against Fascism and Nazi atrocities were suggested as appropriate subjects for publication. At the beginning of 1943, the Committee began to bring back to Moscow a great many of the writers, from places as far apart as Odessa and Tashkent.[279] The Yiddish printing plants were located in the western parts of the country, and were destroyed when the German forces overran this part of the Soviet Union. In the process of a general reorganization of the publishing house Der Emes, a printing plant was established in Moscow, and its director, L. Strongin, became actively engaged in the work of the J.A.C. Given the wartime conditions existing in the Soviet Union, these activities did appear to be a great undertaking.[280]

The publication policies of Der Emes were adjusted to the needs of the prosecution of the war. No anti-religious books or pamphlets were published throughout the duration of the war. A great number of books were published in some cooperation with the J.A.C. These dealt with the impact of the war upon the Jewish people in the Soviet Union. The content and literary quality of the wartime publications were evaluated by an Israeli expert, who stated that "eighty percent of the Yiddish publications of this period were of good Jewish content."[281]

There was a rising demand for the printed word in Yiddish and the sale of books soared. "There were never enough of them on hand." The sale of Yiddish books in the years 1941-1943, alone totalled one million rubles, which meant that at least 100,000 Yiddish books and pamphlets were purchased during this period.[282] Given the need for caution, the officers of the J.A.C. continued to work hard to promote not only the activities already described, but also other cultural activities. Mikhoels, is known to have made numerous efforts to get approval for a wider expansion of the terms of reference of the J.A.C., however, he failed in his efforts. When I arrived in Moscow in November 1944, rumors of such approaches were still being spread among the Committee's employees. In one instance, during my stay in Moscow, Ilya Ehrenburg was supposed to have participated jointly with Mikhoels in an approach to the respective authority.[283]

Jewish and non-Jewish writers were known to have met for literary meetings devoted to good music. Some of these were arranged by the J.A.C., others by the Jewish section of the Ukrainian Academy of Science in Kiev. It is also known that such personalities as K. Simonov, N. Tikhonov, I. Ehrenburg and A. Surkov, attended these literary evenings. Well known artists, such as E. Gillels and D. Oystrakh, also performed on literary evenings. There were also special evenings arranged by writers and artists for particular sections of the Jewish public, such as the Jewish partizans from Belorussia and the Ukraine.[284]

In summary, it can be stated that the origin and function of the J.A.C., was similar to the structure of the four other anti-Fascist committees, whose formation was announced by Lozovsky on April 24, 1942. In performing its functions, the J.A.C. developed certain distinct differences. These differences in organizational purpose, occurred through uncontrolled circumstances, as the extent of the Nazi genocidal policies towards the Jews became increasingly apparent throughout the world. Therefore, Jews in the Soviet Union saw the need for a common bond with other Jews wherever they happened to be, a feeling which transcended state boundaries. When the American Yiddish writer, B.Z. Goldberg, returned for a visit to the Soviet Union in 1946, he compared the activities of the J.A.C. to "a sort of Soviet Jewish Congress."[285] This congressional nature of the J.A.C.'s activities, between 1942 and 1946, appears to have been an accurate assessment. As this chapter has shown, the Committee, despite its narrow term of reference, did attempt to foster world Jewish unity, and it did engage in attempts to strengthen Jewish culture throughout the Soviet Union.

CHAPTER VII

THE JEWISH ANTI-FASCIST COMMITTEE AND WORLD
JEWISH CONGRESS: EFFORTS TOWARDS AFFILIATION

I arrived in Moscow in November 1944, as a member of the Czechoslovak government delegation for the liberated territory of Czechoslovakia. The delegation was formed by the exiled government in London, in accordance with the terms of an agreement, signed between the Soviet Union and Czechoslovakia on May 8, 1944.[286] My assignment was twofold: first, to attend to all matters concerned with the welfare of Czechoslovak Jews in Soviet territory, and second, to undertake, upon return to the liberated territory of Czechoslovakia, the immediate reconstruction of the country's Jewish communities. In addition, I was assigned the task of establishing the groundwork for formal relations between the World Jewish Congress (JWC)[287] and the Jewish Anti-Fascist Committee (J.A.C.).[288] This additional part of the assignment was negotiated by the representatives of the Czechoslovak Jews and the W.J.C., and agreed upon by Jan Masaryk, on behalf of the government of Czechoslovakia.[289] The following description and analysis are limited to the contacts and subsequent negotiations made at that time, which eventually led to the decision of the J.A.C. to cooperate with the W.J.C.

It was a coincidental but fortunate bit of circumstance that my arrival in Moscow coincided with the return to Moscow of the delegate for the liberated territory, Frantisek Nemec. The briefing he gave me about his relations with his Soviet counterparts, proved helpful in gaining insight into the practical aspects of negotiations, with the Communists. His advice was followed very closely in the days ahead, when I made initial contacts with the leaders of the J.A.C.

A few days after my arrival in Moscow, Vladimir Outrata, then the first secretary of the Czechoslovak Embassy, telephoned the J.A.C. to arrange an appointment. At that time, I was introduced over the telephone to

Shakno Epstein, the secretary of the J.A.C., as "the Czech Zionist leader," an oversight, which could have proved to be a serious obstacle to negotiations, but I was relieved when Epstein overlooked it.

A few days later, after more telephone negotiations, an appointment was made for me to meet two senior officials of the J.A.C., Shakno Epstein and Itsik Fefer. Outrata accompanied me to this first meeting. The offices of the J.A.C. were located in a drab, old building at Ulitsa Kropotkina 10, which prior to the revolution of 1917, belonged to the Central Board of Jewish Communities.[290] The conference room was bare of furnishings, except for a long wooden table and two benches. During my first meeting with Epstein[291] and Fefer, I noticed no other activities being conducted on the premises. In stark contrast to my meeting with Mikhoels on the previous evening, in the actors' dressing room at the Jewish State Theater, this first encounter with Epstein and Fefer was rather cool and formal.

Our conversation began with me giving my impressions of the visit of Mikhoels and Fefer to London in the autumn of 1943. We all agreed with Mikhoels's statement, made at that time, that his visit signalled the "end of the isolation of Soviet Jewry."[292] I also referred to a resolution adopted by the National Conference of the British Section of the W.J.C., which stated that "Soviet Jewry should be invited to join the W.J.C."[293] It seemed as if the general climate, created by wartime experiences, was suitable for such a step, not to speak of its desirability from the point of view of Jewish unity, as expressed in the somewhat loose affiliation of many national organizations of Jews, within the W.J.C.

Fefer recalled the meetings he attended in London, and the many conversations he had with representatives of the W.J.C., including, of course, his talks with Dr. L. Zelmanovits, the leader of Czechoslovak Jews. He told me of the pleasure Mikhoels and he had upon receipt of a congratulatory telegram sent by Zelmanovits to the Third Plenum of the J.A.C. on behalf of Czechoslovak Jews.[294]

During this first meeting, I proposed a much closer cooperation between the W.J.C. and the J.A.C. This cooperation was to include an extensive exchange of all publications, periodicals and special issues, as well as lists of surviving Jews and Jewish communities. My proposal was accepted within days, and Epstein notified me of this fact by telephone. I then asked Epstein for authority to communicate this agreement to the W.J.C. in London, through the Czechoslovak Embassy radio service. He agreed and the following cable was sent:

"Had information talks [with] representatives Soviet Jewry Epstein and Fefer stop. Agreed on cooperation, exchange of literature and news stop. Promised documents and material on atrocities against Czechoslovak Jews for Black Book. They agreed [to] attend conference of European Jewry stop. Leaving for Lublin stop. Sending list of surviving Czechoslovak Jews in Poland through C.T.K." [295]

It should also be stated that in December 1944, at the time of these negotiations, the full extent of the Jewish tragedy in Nazi-occupied Europe was not yet revealed, and world Jewry was extremely anxious to obtain some news about relatives and friends who might have survived the Nazi Holocaust. My presence in Moscow soon became known, and I was given numerous lists of survivors by representatives of Polish and Ukrainian Jews, and by American and Polish correspondents who were, in turn, asked by individuals to contact their relatives in the West. I telegraphed these lists to London on a daily basis. The lists of survivors were given top priority at that time. I also received telegrams and letters from London and Jerusalem, containing the names of persons sought by their relatives. These requests were turned over either to the officials of the J.A.C., or to the Czechoslovak Embassy if the request was related to Czechoslovak Jews.

I considered Epstein's quick agreement to the proposed closer cooperation between the W.J.C. and the J.A.C., as an indication of prior approval by the "higher-ups," within the C.P.S.U. Under the circumstances, it could not have been otherwise. Of all the people I encountered, Epstein impressed me most with his strict adherence to whatever he knew to be the party line, at any one particular time. Shortly after the first meeting, I was notified by Zelmanovits of the intention of the British Section of the W.J.C. to convene an Emergency Conference of

European Jewry, and it was suggested that I should try to interest the
J.A.C. to send a delegation. I relayed this suggestion to Epstein, and
within a few days, he informed me that J.A.C. delegates would indeed
be appointed to attend this conference.

The approval of both these suggestions seemed to be indicative of a
consistent policy toward the Jewish people in general, and the J.A.C. in
particular. It appeared then that the same attitude, which prompted
them to send a mission to the Jews in the West in the summer of 1943,
still prevailed.

In the second half of December 1944, I was quite optimistic that I
might accomplish my mission in Moscow with success. Although, he did
not participate in most of my official talks with the J.A.C., I had frequent
conversations with the chairman of the J.A.C., S. Mikhoels. He was a
charming person, hospitable, generous with his time, and a very good lis-
tener. He enquired a lot about Jewish life in Czechoslovakia, and about
the W.J.C., and its leaders in London. Mikhoels, expressed an optimistic
outlook on the future of the Jewish people, and this boundless optimism
combined with his excellent personality, left a marked influence on me.

During the first week of January 1945, we resumed the negotiations
at the offices of the J.A.C. Epstein, dealt with the proposed participation
of the first postwar European Conference of the W.J.C., and made this
participation conditional upon the agreement of the W.J.C. to three
stipulations. First, the J.A.C. had to participate in drafting and approv-
ing the conference agenda. Second, the J.A.C. had to obtain an equal
number of delegates with the rest of world Jewry combined. Third,
there was a demand for an equal share in the representation on all
W.J.C. bodies, such as the executive, the secretariat, and the resolution
and political committees. This last condition, referred to in our talks as
the fifty-fifty condition, was also raised by Epstein in connection with
the terms of the planned affiliation with the W.J.C. The demand created
serious difficulties in negotiations, because it implied a complete
restructuring of the W.J.C.

I foresaw real difficulties in trying to affect this condition, and I
explained how the composition of such a voluntary organization as the
W.J.C. would make a fifty-fifty division along the lines proposed difficult,
if not impossible. I also explained how the executive of the W.J.C., is

elected, and that most decision-making was done by agreement. A formula on representation is usually agreed upon in relation to the respective numerical strength of a national community, so that equal representation can be preserved. The choice of the headquarters in the United States was due, in part, to the numerical strength of American Jewry, but also due to the favorable conditions under which the World Jewish Congress was operating there.[296] Fefer monopolized most of the conversation, and repeatedly stated that the third condition was a fair one to insist upon, because of the numerical strength of the Jews in the U.S.S.R.[297] By this time, all of us present at these meetings knew something of the tragedy which had befallen Soviet Jewry, but we were still ignorant of the full extent of this catastrophe. Somehow, we still hoped that when all the facts were known, the losses would not be so heavy. Therefore, the point of numerical equality was neither questioned nor discussed, because everyone concerned hoped the official figures would still remain largely valid.

Both sides of the negotiating table were fully aware that there was another important aspect of division between the Soviet Jews and the remainder of world Jewry. But at no time during the negotiations were the ideological differences brought into the open. This control of the ideological viewpoint was due, in large measure, to Fefer's determination to keep the lines of communication between the W.J.C. and the J.A.C. open. Having raised the three conditions to a formal affiliation, Epstein said little in the ensuing debate, and it was difficult to form an impression of his personal attitude. However, both Epstein and Fefer expressed the hope that they would be part of the Soviet Jewish delegation to the proposed conference of European Jewry. Fefer suggested Prague, for instance, as a possible conference site, and thought its central location would make it a popular location for many to participate. I left this meeting convinced that some means would be found to overcome the difficulties raised, and that through actual participation in a conference, a suitable compromise solution would occur. The most important aspect was to actually achieve the participation of Soviet Jewry in the proposed conference.

Thereupon, I sent a lengthy report of the negotiations to the British section of the W.J.C., addressed to Jan Masaryk, and another report to Rabbi S.S. Wise. In view of my short visit to Moscow, I requested not only a prompt reply, but full instructions as to how I should proceed in the negotiations. For the next ten days while I was in Moscow, a reply was not forthcoming. An indirect response to my report reached me in a letter from Dr. Zelmanovits, of the British section of the W.J.C., but this had arrived too late to be of any practical use in my negotiations with the J.A.C.

Among other things, the letter from Dr. Zelmanovits, expressed the hope that Soviet Jewry would be represented in the proposed conference:

> "We expect their participation. Your report and the content of your talks with Fefer and Epstein are very valuable. I wish that Czechoslovak Jewry would be represented as well." [298]

But I had already moved on to the other important considerations of my mission. I was then primarily concerned with establishing an organization to assist and to absorb Jewish survivors of the concentration camps, from the eastern section of Poland and from Austria.

Negotiations to stage this conference and bring about some "meeting of minds" between Soviet Jewry and Jews in other parts of the world, were never resumed. The proposed conference in Prague did not materialize, but some exchange of information on survivors between Moscow, on the one hand, and London and New York, on the other, continued. However, correspondence could not replace personal contact. A resumé of the endeavors to continue the negotiations and contacts by other methods of communication is contained in a lengthy report of one of the participants. The following extract from the report is indicative of the efforts made by the W.J.C.:

> "Both we in New York and our British Section tried to arrange a meeting with the leaders of the J.A.C. in Prague or Paris or some other agreeable place. We did not succeed. We invited them to attend some of our international meetings. These invitations were politely received, but there was some other vague commitment which prevented acceptance. It was obvious in general that

we were dealing with unseen factors, and my own view is that one or another of these invitations would have been accepted if the leaders of the J.A.C. had been free to do so." [299]

Perlzweig's explanation, particularly in the last sentence, would suggest that by the end of the Second World War, the Soviet policy towards the Jews had changed. No longer was it necessary to identify the hopes and aspirations of Soviet Jewry with those of Jews all over the world, because the Nazi threat was now a spent force. In addition, a new element entered into the relations between the wartime allies, particularly between the Soviet Union and the United States. It acted from the beginning as a disruptive force, and before long, an era of distrust began to make an appearance. Whether this was one of the "unseen factors" described in Perlzweig's summary, remains questionable because of lack of documentary evidence, and because the J.A.C. actually increased its operations after the war.

In 1946, Goldberg visited the J.A.C., and found it a "big undertaking." [300] It functioned on an international basis which, from the Soviet point of view, was its original and prime purpose. But it also operated "like a civilian organ of the Soviet Jewish community" and, as Goldberg told S.A. Lozovsky, "it seemed to be developing into a sort of Soviet Jewish Congress, like the American Jewish Congress." [301] However, my assessment of the J.A.C. in the fall of 1944, differed from that given by Goldberg. By 1946, the operations of the J.A.C. were being conducted on a much more expanded scale. It must be remembered that 1946 was the anniversary of the death of Sholom Alechem, the great and popular Russian Yiddish writer, and its observance in Moscow was held in the Hall of Columns. [302] Goldberg, was undoubtedly influenced by the festive spirit staged for this occasion. His name, appearing on the public posters, bore the identification "from America," indicating this connection was being advertised for all it was worth. Later he was to reflect on the anniversary meeting:

"The greatest public cultural achievement of the Jewish Anti-Fascist Committee inside Russia, which turned out to be the last

cultural event in the life of the Soviet Jewish community — the
swan song of Yiddish culture — was the observance of the thir-
tieth anniversary of the death of Sholom Aleichem." [303]

However, the J.A.C. continued to function without any apparent
substantial changes. Goldberg, accompanied by Fefer, made extensive
trips throughout the Soviet Union. He felt that Fefer wanted to impress
upon various local officials that:

"... Jews were influential in the United States, and that they were
interested in the fate of the Jews in the Soviet Union.
Consciously or subconsciously, Fefer seemed to feel the interest
of American Jewry in the Jews of the Soviet Union was an asset,
an additional element of security." [304]

Thus, at a time when the Soviet Union was moving away from close
cooperation with its Western allies, the J.A.C., in Goldberg's interpretation, moved in the other direction. Herein lies part of the explanation
for the tragedy that followed in November 1948. The J.A.C. was caught
in the horns of a dilemma. On the one hand, it desired to continue the
improvement of relations with the American Jewry, and indeed with
Jews all over the world. On the other hand, it had to comply with the
strict directives laid down by the Party, directives which changed rapidly as the international scene changed. Expediency no longer dictated
the cultivation of American Jewry. Therefore, the lack of cooperation
with the W.J.C. in the New York Black Book Committee venture and
the poor response to the many invitations to international meetings of
the W.J.C., were indicative of a change of policy. Yet, in 1947, when a
member of the Swedish section of the W.J.C. visited the office of the
J.A.C., he was told in unequivocal terms by G. Heifetz, the acting
secretary, that the "representation of Soviet Jews for the proposed
General Assembly Meeting of the W.J.C. in 1948 was inadequate." [305]
Therefore, it seems that the question of numerical representation, as
one of the main conditions of affiliation, persisted long after the inter-
ruption of my negotiations with the J.A.C. In 1947, there was no

longer any doubt that the numerical equality between the American Jewry and Soviet Jewry, did not exist. There seems likely another reason for Soviet insistence on adequate representation; namely, the desire to control the W.J.C., and to use it to further Soviet interests. Such reasoning, coincided with the short period of experimenting with Soviet techniques of control, among the People's Democracies of Central and Eastern Europe.

CHAPTER VIII

THE DEMISE OF THE JEWISH ANTI-FASCIST COMMITTEE AND YIDDISH CULTURE

The chain of events, which led to the dissolution of the J.A.C. and to the liquidation of Yiddish writers in the Soviet Union, developed over a period of three years, and was mainly due to events outside the borders of the Soviet Union. The origin of these events seemed to have occurred in the Soviet appraisal of the American refusal of January 1945, to grant the Soviet Union a postwar reconstruction loan, and in President Truman's abrupt termination of lend-lease shipments.[306] Stalin's interpretation of both these American decisions,[307] left no doubt that the existing close relationship of cooperation between the two wartime allies, should be terminated.

The consequences of this sudden reversal were not immediately apparent in domestic Soviet policies, and could not be deduced from the actions of the leaders of the J.A.C. On the contrary, the scope of the activities of the Committee was increased. This occurred particularly in the domestic sphere, and was beyond the original terms of reference announced at the time of the formation of the J.A.C. There were a few instances, when this policy of increased activity seemed to be held in question, but generally it was felt that these were exceptional instances when other specific considerations were involved. For instance, the two Yiddish publishing houses in Kiev and Minsk were not re-established, and the publishing program of the Moscow Der Emes was discarded.[308] On the other hand, the sudden revival of the Birobidzhan project pointed in the opposite direction. This revival was officially announced by the Central Committee of Obkom C. P., of Birobidzhan. In a decree published on January 26, 1946, the Party addressed itself "specifically to the Jews," and called "for renewed efforts in developing the Jewish Autonomous Region."[309] The leaders of the J.A.C. were ostensibly unaware of any change of policy, and

Fefer, in particular, made plans for a postwar program in the international field of activities. He designed a plan, which he thought would be vital to Soviet interests, and would also ensure the continued existence of the J.A.C.

The plan foresaw a world Jewish conference to be convened by the J.A.C. to discuss three basic issues. These were "… the continued struggle against Fascism, steps to be taken against anti-Semitism, and the problem of Palestine."[310] Fefer thought two of the issues, namely the fight against Fascism and anti-Semitism, would put the Soviet Union in a particularly favorable position in the eyes of progressive world opinion, because the Soviet Union would be seen as the vanguard of this struggle. The third issue, that of Palestine, would enable the Soviet Union to be "invited" into the Middle East region. It would also give her a seat at a conference table of the big powers, who thus far were ignoring her in any discussions of matters relating to Palestine or the Middle East. "Whatever its motive," wrote Goldberg, "such a conference would have made the Soviet Jews part of the World Jewry." It appears now that none of the activities of the J.A.C., whether in the domestic field or in the area of international propaganda, was consistent with the trends developing in Soviet foreign relations.

Three consecutive Soviet requests for postwar assistance (the loan request, the continuation of lend-lease and the demand for West German reparations), were either turned down or left pending by the government of the United States. The Soviet leaders misinterpreted the motives for the refusals (for instance, they disregarded the fact that Britain was equally affected by the lend-lease cancellation), and assumed that "the West was resuming its old course of capitalist encirclement."[311] Therefore, the Cold War was started and "began to acquire a cumulative momentum."[312] Stalin's own reaction was given to A. Harriman, at Sochi, in October 1945, when he was quoted as saying that "the Soviet Union was going isolationist."[313]

Soviet isolationism could only have meant a sharp break from such ongoing policies as the cooperation between former wartime allies and cooperation within international bodies. The break with both these concepts was bound to have very serious ramifications not only inside the Soviet Union, but also inside the People's Republics forming the outer ring of the Soviet Union in the West. There was a certain amount of vacillation in Soviet foreign policy, and a certain amount of experimenting with techniques of control in Eastern Europe. In March 1947, at the foreign ministers conference in Moscow, the Americans still had hopes for a modus vivendi with the Soviet Union. Three months later, the Soviet Union and the countries of Eastern Europe, accepted the American invitation to participate in the Marshall Plan conference, held in Paris, on July 2, 1947. "The point of no return came," wrote Schlessinger, "when Molotov after bringing 89 technical specialists with him to Paris and evincing initial interest, received the hot flash from the Kremlin, denounced the whole idea, and walked out of the conference."[314] The cooperation of the Soviet Union with the United States was at an end, and for the next decade, the world was essentially divided into two hostile camps.

It was quite natural to expect that the Soviet Union's return to isolationism would have tremendous repercussions on its domestic scene. The initial reaction came in the form of an outburst against "Western bourgeois influences," and shortly thereafter the Central Committee of the C.P.S.U. called for the return to "Socialist realism" in arts and literature. The influential member of the Politburo, A.A. Zhdanov, began a campaign against all those "monthlies, which published writers who had no place in Soviet society and its literature."[315] The attack was general, for it was directed against all Soviet writers, who did not conform, and who disclosed "Western bourgeois" influences. Among others, the known Soviet writers M. Zoshchenko and A. Akhmatova, were strongly denounced. N.S. Krushchev, in a speech at a plenary session of the Central Committee of the Ukrainian Communist Party, was quoted as condemning "... ideological errors, distortions, and attempts at reviving bourgeois nationalist concepts."[316] The Jewish leadership in the J.A.C., as it is known, consisted almost exclusively of writers, poets and artists. Nearly all of them were known to have had contacts abroad, particularly in the United States. The revival of these contacts was considered a useful asset to the Soviet Union during the war, but the situation was changing in 1947. What was an asset became a treasonable activity. Therefore, shortly after he launched his campaign to rid the Soviet Union of bourgeois influences, Zhdanov's attack began to assume anti-Semitic overtones when his criticisms were "whipped up against them under the guise of cosmopolitans.[317] Later, cosmopolitans were identified as Jews, who were "passportless vagabonds, gypsies without a fatherland."[318] The move to liquidate Yiddish writers, Yiddish literature and the J.A.C. was now in earnest, and could be traced through distinct stages.

It all began with the "automobile accident" in Minsk, on January 13, 1948, in which Mikhoels was murdered by the M.G.B. "It was part of the conspiracy against Yiddish culture and the Jewish people," wrote one writer.[319] It was Ehrenburg who years later called the automobile accident a murder and told an American writer that Mikhoels's death was followed by the arrests of a large number of Jewish writers, and the beginning of the process of wiping out the record of Jewish martyrdom and heroism in World War II.[320]

The actions against the Jews were designed on a large scale, and developed in broad outlines to include a series of plots, all interrelated, and made public at different times, to embrace all the "criminal" activities the Jews were accused of. Some plots were designed for "intra-Party consumption and for the People's Democracies,"[321] while others were to prepare the mass of Soviet peoples for the final stage, namely, the liquidation of the Jewish writers grouped around the J.A.C. The atmosphere in the U.S.S.R. in the summer of 1948 was such that "Stalin anticipated the possibility of war with the United States and was considering what to do with Russian Jewry in the event that the war broke out."[322] Stalin was supposedly "toying with the idea of deporting all Jews to Siberia, but his comrades in the Politburo opposed this, fearing it would enrage the world against the Soviet Union."[323] With this as a background, the first of the plots charged the leaders of the J.A.C., with conspiracy to "have the Crimea designated as a Jewish Autonomous Region in order to convert it into an American military base."[324] Therefore, Jews, particularly those active within the J.A.C., were identified with potential treasonable activities, against the Soviet Union. However, the net was spread wide apart to include Svetlana

Alliluyeva's former father-in-law, I.G. Morozov, Molotov's wife, and many others in Stalin's disfavor.[325] In fact, Stalin was to categorize all Jews as dangerous Zionists, therefore beginning a trend that seems to have survived to this day. Svetlana Alliluyeva is quoted as telling her father, "It made no sense to accuse her former father-in-law of Zionism," but Stalin retorted angrily: "No! You don't understand. The entire older generation is contaminated with Zionism, and now they are teaching the young people, too."[326] The charge that all Jews were potential traitors was reinforced in a subsequent plot against Jewish intellectuals from Birobidzhan. They were collectively accused of a "dual conspiracy to impose Jewish rule over the non-Jews of the region, and to turn it over to Japan as a base against the Soviet Union."[327] Finally, there was the "doctors' plot," in which Jewish physicians, among others, were accused of a conspiracy to poison the leaders of the Soviet Union. In this charge, a link was shown to have existed to the "Joint,"[328] and to the J.A.C. through Mikhoels's close family relationship to one of the accused, Dr. Vofsi. Some of these charges extended to Jews in high Party positions, in the People's Democracies.[329]

All these plots were advertised through the news media, with the intention of obtaining the widest publicity. In this aspect, the atmosphere created in the Soviet Union, did not differ much from that in Nazi Germany in the earlier stages of the anti-Jewish policies. Just as Jews in Germany were stripped of their rights to continue in their professions, Soviet Jewish writers also lost their membership in the Union of Soviet Writers. "The procedure was to read the names of the people regarded as unfit to be continued in membership," explained Goldberg, "the names being all Jewish and no one questioning the reason or challenging the suggestion."[330] The move was apparently stopped by Ilya Ehrenburg, when he asked why his name was omitted from the list.[331]

The last issue of *Aynikayt* appeared on November 20, 1948, and a few days later the J.A.C. was dissolved. Within the next two months, hundreds of people were arrested, among them the leading writers and intellectuals in the J.A.C. Prominent Communists, such as the official responsible for the activities of the J.A.C., Solomon Lozovsky, the rabbi of the Moscow synagogue, Schlieffer, and its president, Khobrutsky,[332] were arrested in this massive drive, extending from Moscow to Birobidzhan, to wipe out Jewish intellectuals and potential leaders. Fear and panic spread among the Soviet Jews. It was all part of a scheme to "solve the Jewish problem" by a "madman's decision":

> "Stalin, decided [Ehrenburg said to Schneiderman] he would decapitate the leadership of the Jews — their poets, artists, scientists — and the great mass of frightened, bewildered Jews would thus be cowed."[333]

Once the Jewish leaders were liquidated, the problem of the Jewish nationality would be considered solved, and Jews "would be declared nonexistent!"[334] This is what actually happened. In the meantime, it took eight years of insistent inquiries to confirm that the Jewish intellectuals were executed, on August 12, 1952.[335] They were never rehabilitated either individually, or collectively, as members of the J.A.C. The attitude of *"krome yevreyev"* ("except the Jews"),[336] persisted long after the de-Stalinization period was introduced. It seems to prevail to this day.

CONCLUSION

The Jewish Anti-Fascist Committee (J.A.C.) came into being as a result of the 1942 German attack upon Soviet Russia. The Soviet government viewed the aggression with apprehension and mobilized all its material resources for the defence of the fatherland. The choice of the Jewish nationality, one among many other minority nationalities in the Soviet Union, as a possible vehicle for foreign contacts and the influencing of public opinion abroad, lay in the fact of a Jewish diaspora, and in an overestimation of "Jewish influence" in America and in England. One Soviet announcement said in reference to the J.A.C.:

> "Jews have formed an Anti-Fascist Committee in order to help the Soviet Union, England and the United States to put an end to the bloodthirsty rage of Hitler and other Fascist apes who fancy themselves as a master race."[337]

This statement gives the impression that the Committee was formed on the initiative of Soviet Jews, and subsequently, approved by the Party and government. Such an initiative is highly doubtful in the Soviet political system. It appears from the evidence given by some experts (Goldberg and Aronson, among others), that a number of leading Soviet Jews were in fact ordered to join the J.A.C. (for example, Ehrenburg, Zaslavsky, Bregman, and Generals Kaizer and Katz). From the evidence so far divulged, it appears that the J.A.C. was to be a propaganda vehicle for international purposes, and it was to be controlled by the Party.

Jewish writers, poets, artists and intellectuals associated with the J.A.C. soon realized the necessity to broaden the scope of the Committee's activities so as to foster cultural and national aspirations of Jews in the Soviet Union. Between 1942 and 1944, the J.A.C. became an important organization, not only within the Soviet Union, but also to world Jewry, which began to pay serious attention to its activities. It is primarily for this reason that I was commissioned to hold preliminary negotiations with J.A.C. representatives, during my official visit to Moscow in 1944.

Also, as a result of personal contacts established during the visit of the J.A.C. mission to America and England in 1943, a mutual desire was expressed by both the World Jewish Congress and J.A.C. officials for closer ties between the two bodies. All of these preliminary soundings never came to full fruition. Reasons for this are still speculative, but my assessment as an interested observer leads me to believe that as the Cold War began, Soviet designs for the J.A.C. changed: no longer was it necessary to influence Jewish communities in England and the United States of America. The J.A.C. was judged as redundant and Stalin began his mass liquidation of its officials. Not only was the J.A.C. judged as redundant, but it now became increasingly suspected of being a subversive tool of Zionists, allied with the United States against the USSR. The J.A.C.'s attempts at negotiations and its expansion into the cultural and social fields of activity indicated that the Jewish intelligencia at war's end were not assimilated, but continued to be aware of their cultural and national heritage. The study of the development of Soviet Jewish cultural identity and national heritage is still very much in its exploratory stages. As such, this thesis makes no great claim of analyzing all the relevant information on this organization. Much is still unknown, and perhaps will never be known. However, it is hoped that this short analysis would have given some clues as to why the Jewish minority question continues to be a "problem" today in the Soviet Union.

APPENDIX

Commissar of Internal Affairs
of the Soviet Union, L.P. Beria!

Dear Lavrenti Pavlovich!

My department had a number of consultations in order to work out
the principles we agreed upon in our recent communication with
you. The result of the consultations is a submission of the initiating
group to the Chairman of the Council of People's Commissars in
regard to the foundation of a Jewish Anti-Hitlerite Committee, with
a request to permit the establishment of such a committee on the
territory of the Soviet Union.

Attached is a copy of our submission.

At the same time, we turn to you with a request, dear Lavrenti
Pavlovich, so that we come to a positive decision.

With socialist greetings,

Erlich

Alter

Moscow, …. October, 1941.

[Translated from the Yiddish text as reproduced in Unser Tsait, No. 7,
July 1943, p. 26, by Dr. I. Rosenberg.]

ENDNOTES

1 Ben Zion Goldberg, The Jewish Problem in the Soviet Union (New York: Crown Publishers Inc., 1961), p. 1.

2 Herman Rosenthal, "Russia," The Jewish Encyclopedia, Vol, 10 (New York: Funk and Wagnalls, Co., 1905), p. 526.

3 Ibid., p. 526.

4 Ibid.

5 Ibid.,p . 523.

6 Herman Rosenthal, "Pale of Settlement," The Jewish Encyclopedia, Vol. 9, p. 468.

7 Ibid.

8 Shmarya Levin, cited in Maurice Samuel, ed., Forward from Exile (Philadelphia: The Jewish Publication Society of America, 1967), p. 287.

9 Ibid., p. 288.

10 It can even be argued upon with some justification that the existence of the Bund contributed substantially to the formulation of Lenin's concept of a socialist party of nationalities.

11 Leonard Stein, ed., The Letters and Papers of Chaim Weizman, Vol. 1 (London: Oxford University Press, 1968), p. 210.

12 Levin, op cit., p. 296.

13 Ibid., p. 297.

14 Ibid., p. 397.

15 Ibid., p. 377.

16 Ibid., p. 397.

17 Ibid.

18 Ibid., p. 376.

19 Ibid., p. 356.

20 For example, Lenin derogatively referred to the Jewish socialists of the Bund as "Separatists and Liquidators." See his "Separatists in Russia and Separatists in Austria," in Lenin on the Jewish Question (New York: International Publishers Co., Inc., 1934), p. 20.

21 Shmarya Levin, cited in Maurice Samuel, ed., Forward from Exile (Philadelphia: The Jewish Publication Society of America, 1967), p. 401.

[22] The Black Hundreds was the popular name for the organization known as League of the Russian People, founded in 1904. It was headed by Dr. Dubrovin, Purishkevich, Markov and numerous government and police officials. On December 23, 1905, Tsar Nicholas II said to a delegation: "Unite the Russian people. I count on you." See M. Vishniak, "Antisemitism in Tsarist Russia," in K.S. Pinson, ed., Essays on Antisemitism (New York: (publisher not cited), 1946), p. 138.

[23] Levin, op. cit., p. 401.

[24] Herman Rosenthal, "Russia," The Jewish Encyclopedia, Vol, 10 (New York: Funk and Wagnalls Co., 1905), p. 528.

[25] S.M. Dubnov, History of Jews in Russia and Poland, Vol. 3 (Philadelphia: The Jewish Publication Society of America, 1920), p. 110-111.

[26] Ibid., p. 110.

[27] This does not mean that Witte's government did anything positive to defend Jews against the organized mobs. Dubnov, for instance, claims that Witte's government "issues official statements on the pogroms, which are based on the fabricated reports invented by the very government officials who had instigated or organized them." See S.M. Dubnov, "The Moral of Stormy Days," in K.S. Pinson, ed., Nationalism and History (Philadelphia: The Jewish Publication Society of America, 1958), p. 202.

[28] Ibid., p. 107.

[29] Ibid., p. 110.

[30] Levin, op. cit., p. 402.

[31] Pinson, op. cit., p. 372.

[32] Excerpt for the boycott of the election by the Bund.

[33] Levin, op cit., p. 400.

[34] Vinaver was also one of the leaders of the Constitutional Democratic Party.

[35] Simon Markovich Dubnov was a prominent Jewish historian, political writer and, at one time, leader of a Jewish political party in Russia, the "Folkspartay." The more important of his works were: History of the Jews in Russia and Poland, World History of the Jewish People, school textbooks on Jewish history, and History of the Hasidim. His theory of diaspora nationalism has influenced Jewish thinking. Unlike Graetz, his predecessor in the field of Jewish history, Dubnov maintained that the existence of Jewish people does not depend on culture and religion alone, but also on communal organization in the diaspora. He was in sympathy with Zionism, but

did not think that Jewish unity depends upon national territory or an independent state. He declared that Jewish minority groups should be considered as national groups, entitled to cultural and communal autonomy.

[36] Sidney Harcave, "The Jews and the First Russian National Election," The
American Slavic & East European Review ,Vol. 9, 1950, p. 34.

[37] Ibid., p. 34.

[38] Pinson, op. cit., p. 212.

[39] Ibid.

[40] Harcave, op. cit., p. 25.

[41] Ibid.

[42] Levin, op. cit., p. 408.

[43] Ibid. Harcave states that it was Dubnov who suggested a Jewish parliamentary faction (p. 35) and caused a "disagreement." This conflicts with the
above interpretation which follows, essentially that given by deputy Levin.

[44] Ibid., p. 410.

[45] This, of course, omits the small proportion of Jewish Socialists, who desired
total destruction of the political system.

[46] One of the levers of government control was the "state rabbi," a cleric who
had to undergo a Russian-approved educational training, and who, upon
his graduation, was used to control the community. This cleric, became
derogatively known as "scapegoat" rabbi, and he had neither standing nor
respect in the Jewish community.

[47] Dubnov's concept of national autonomy was accepted by the peace makers
in 1919, and incorporated into the provisions for the protection of national
minorities, in the peace treaties, with the succession states. This program of
national autonomy, called for autonomous administration of Hebrew and
Yiddish schools, scientific and cultural institutions, publishing houses and
periodicals. Among its political demands, the Folkspartay advocated full self-
government in the cultural field and democratic elections to all representative bodies.

[48] The Bund was founded in Vilna in 1897. At its Sixth Convention in Zurich
(1905), the Bund adopted a program of civil and political emancipation, and
a national-cultural autonomy for the Jewish people. As a workers' party it
fought for Russian political demands and for specific rights of Jewish workers. At the beginning of 1905, the Russian Social Democratic Party had 8,400
members, the Bund had 25,000.

The United Party was formed by a merger of two parties: the Zionist-Socialist (S.S.) and the Sejmists, so called, because of their advocacy of an elected National Assembly. By 1917, the United Party had 13,000 members. The Poale Zion was a Palestine-oriented Marxist-Zionist group, formed in 1901. A youth group occupied an intermediate position with no stress on class struggle and with a non-Marxist ideological concept. Many of its members emigrated to Palestine, and subsequently provided many of that country's political leaders.

[49] Dubnov, in Pinson, op. cit., p. 138.

[50] T.B. Schechtman, "The USSR, Zionism, and Israel," in Lionel Kochan, ed., The Jews in Soviet Russia Since 1917 (London: Oxford University Press, 1970), p. 101.

[51] N.P. Ignatev became minister of the interior on the assassination of Alexander II. He was the author of the notorious "May Laws," and used his influence to promote anti-Jewish legislation.

[52] Rosenthal, op. cit., p. 528.

[53] Dubnov, in Pinson, op. cit., p. 202.

[54] Rosenthal, op. cit., p. 529.

[55] Ibid., p. 527.

[56] Ibid., p. 529.

[57] Cited by Dubnov, in Pinson, op. cit., p. 218.

[58] Ibid.

[59] Ibid., p. 140.

[60] Levin, op. cit., p 352.

[61] Ibid.

[62] Rosenthal, op. cit., p. 528.

[63] Levin, op. cit., p. 396.

[64] Gregor Aronson, "Jewish Communal Life in 1917-1918," in Russian Jewry 1917-1967 (New York: Thomas Yoseloff, 1969), p. 17.

[65] S. Ettinger, "The Jews in Russia at the Outbreak of the Revolution," in Kochan, ed., op. cit., p. 26.

[66] Aronson, op. cit., p. 14.

[67] See footnote 6, p. 13.

[68] Ettinger, op. cit., p. 26.

[69] Guido G. Goldman, Zionism Under Soviet Rule (New York: Herzl Press, 1960), p. 31.

[70] Karl Marx, Early Writings, translated and edited by T.B. Bottomore (New York: McGraw-Hill Book Co., 1963), p. 3.

[71] Ibid., p. v.

[72] For instance, P.E. Lavrov, T.G. Masaryk, S.M. Dubnov and J. Miller, among many others.

[73] Marx, op. cit., p. 3.

[74] Ibid.

[75] Jacob Miller, "Soviet Theory on Jews," in L, Kochan, ed., The Jews in Soviet Russia Since 1917 (London: Oxford University Press, 1970), p. 47.

[76] Richard Pipes, The Formation of the Soviet Union (Cambridge: Harvard University Press, 1964), p. 22.

[77] Ibid., p. 21.

[78] See article by Lenin on "Separatists in Russia and Separatists in Austria," in Lenin on the Jewish Question (New York: International Publishers Co. Inc., 1934), p. 20.

[79] Pipes, op. cit., p. 25.

[80] Ibid., p. 21.

[81] "Moreover," wrote Pipes, "the basic assumption on which Marx and Engels had founded their belief in the eventual disappearance of nationalism was obviously incorrect." Ibid., p. 22.

[82] Ibid., p. 24.

[83] bid., p. 25.

[84] Solomon M. Schwarz, The Jews in the Soviet Union (Syracuse: Syracuse University Press, 1951), p. 57.

[85] Robert Conquest, ed., Soviet Nationalities Policy in Practice (London: The Bodley Head Ltd., 1967), p. 7.

[86] Schwarz, op. cit., p. 57.

[87] Samad Shaheen, The Communist Theory of National Self-Determination (The Hague: W. Van Hoeve Ltd., 1956), p. 24. Italics added for emphasis.

[88] Ibid.

[89] Pipes, op. cit., p. 32.

[90] Ibid.

[91] Cited in Pinson, op. cit., p. 26.

[92] Cited in Pipes, op. cit., p. 36.

[93] Schwarz, op. cit., p. 53.

[94] Ibid., p. 37.

[95] Ibid., p. 38.

[96] Miller, op. cit., p. 49.

[97] Ibid., p. 49.

[98] Ibid., p. 49.

[99] Lenin on "National Culture," in Lenin on the Jewish Question, p. 13.

[100] Ibid., p. 13.

[101] Pipes, op. cit., p. 43.

[102] Ibid., p. 44.

[103] Ibid., p. 45.

[104] Solomon M. Schwarz, The Jews in the Soviet Union (Syracuse: Syracuse University Press, 1951), p. 50.

[105] T.B. Schechtman, "The USSR, Zionism, and Israel," in L. Kochan, ed., The Jews in Soviet Russia Since 1917 (London: Oxford University Press, 1970), p. 101.

[106] William Korey, "The Legal Position of Soviet Jewry," in Kochan, ed., op. cit., p. 76.

[107] Salo W. Baron, The Russian Jew Under Tsars and Soviets (New York: The Macmillan Company, 1964), p. 206.

[108] Robert Conquest, ed., Soviet Nationalities Policy in Practice (London: The Bodley Read Ltd., 1967), p. 22.

[109] Baron, op. cit., p. 206.

[110] Schwarz, op. cit., p. 97.

[111] Z.Y Gitelman, "The Jewish Sections of the Communist Party and the Modernization of Soviet Jewry," unpublished Ph.D thesis (New York: Columbia University, 1968), microfilm, p. i.

[112] Lenin on the Jewish Question (New York: International Publishers Co. Inc., 1934), p. 23. Lenin was then Chairman of the Council of People's Commissars, and Stalin was the People's Commissar for Nationality Affairs.

[113] Ibid.

[114] Gitelman called this temporary respite an "abdication of Party responsibility to the Sections." Op. cit., p.i.

[115] Joshua Rothenberg, "Jewish Religion in the Soviet Union," in Kochan, ed., op. cit., p. 161.

[116] Lenin on the Jewish Question, p. 23.

[117] Baron, op. cit., p. 209.

[118] Schwarz, op, cit., pp 111-112.

[119] Melech Epstein, The Jew and Communism (New York: Trade Union Sponsoring Committee, 1959), p. 161.

[120] Ibid., p. 160.

[121] Ibid., p. 161.

[122] Ibid., p. 106.

[123] Rothenberg, op. cit., p. 163.

[124] The declassed strata of Jews, generally comprised of businessmen, small traders, some professionals and manufacturers.

[125] A term used by S.M. Dubnov in an address in Kovno, Lithuania, in 1935. He said: "In Russia the Jew is passing through the furnace of de-historization. Jewish history is not taught there, our past is viewed as disgusting and trivial." Cited in Benjamin West, Struggles of a Generation (Tel Aviv, Massada Publishing Co., 1959), p. 111.

[126] Individuals, such as Trotsky, Zinoviev, Kamenev and others, in fact, considered themselves Russians, and were not interested in Jewish matters or problems, affecting Jewish people.

[127] Guido G. Goldman, Zionism under Soviet Rule (1917-1928) (New York: Herzl Press, 1960), p. 36.

[128] Ibid., p. 37.

[129] Schechtman, loc. cit., p. 112.

[130] Baron, op. cit., p. 213. [Italics added for emphasis.]

[131] Ozet was a non-official society for the promotion of Jewish agricultural settlements; the leaders of the society were, however, members of the Komzet, the government organ established by a decree of the Central Executive committee of the U.S.S.R., on August 29, 1924.

[132] Solomon S. Schwarz, "Birobidzhan," in Jacob Frumkin et al., eds., Russian Jewry 1917-1967 (New York: Thomas Yoseloff, 1969), p. 344.

[133] Ibid., p. 347.

[134] Ibid., p. 344.

[135] Baron, op. cit., p. 225.

[136] Alex Nove and J.A. Newth, "The Jewish Population Demographic Trends and Occupational Patterns," in Kochan, ed., op. cit., p. 125.

[137] Schwarz, The Jews-in the Soviet Union, p. 298.

[138] This amounted to about twenty-five titles.

[139] Agrojoint—an organization financed by the American Joint Distribution Committee (popularly known as Joint), supporting agricultural settlements

and rural colonization of Jews in Soviet Russia; ORT (Organization for Rehabilitation through Training) organizes and maintains vocational training schools throughout the world.

[140] Gregor Aronson, "The Jewish Question in the Stalin Era," in Frumkin et al., eds., op. cit., pp. 180-162.

[141] William Korey, "The Legal Position of Soviet Jewry," in L. Kochan, ed., The Jews in Soviet Russia since 1917 (London: Oxford University Press, 1970), p. 78.

[142] Alex Nove and T.A. Newth, "The Jewish Population: Demographic Jews and Occupational Patterns," in Kochan, ed., op. cit., p. 138-139; Salo W. Baron, The Russian Jew Under Tsars and Soviets (New York: The Macmillan Co., 1964), p. 294; Schwarz cited a table showing an approximate total of 1.9 million, Solomon M. Schwarz, The Jews in the Soviet Union (Syracuse: Syracuse University Press, 1951), p. 219. With a few exceptions, wrote Schwarz, those Jewish inhabitants of the invaded regions, who stayed behind when the Red Army retreated, were exterminated. Also, Reuben Ainsztein, "Soviet Jewry in the Second World War," in Kochan, ed., op. cit., p. 274.

[143] New York Times, July 9, 1943. However, at this time, it was known that at least a million Jews perished, during the swift German advances in the first six months after Germany attacked the Soviet Union.

[144] Author's report to World Jewish Congress in London.

[145] Isaac Deutscher, The Non-Jewish Jew and Other Essays (New York: Oxford University Press, 1968), p. 77.

[146] Ibid., p. 78.

[147] Ben Zion Goldberg, The Jewish Problem in the Soviet Union (New York: Crown Publication Inc., 1961), p. 51. Hofstein, was himself later executed with other Jewish writers and poets in 1952.

[148] Ibid., p. 51.

[149] Ibid., p. 52.

[150] See Arthur Koestler's preface to M. Buber-Neumann's study on the Czech journalist Milena Jesenska, in Mistress to Kafka (London: Seeker and Warburg Ltd., 1966), p. 11.

[151] Deutscher, op. cit., p. 77.

[152] Goldberg, op. cit., p. 306.

[153] Ch. Szmeruk. "Yiddish Publications in the U.S.S.R.," Yad Washem Studies,

vol. 4, Jerusalem, 1960, p, 110.

154 Ibid., p. 110-111.

155 Ilya Ehrenburg, Memoirs 1921-1941 (New York: Grosset and Dunlap, 1966). p. 499.

156 Ibid.

157 Ibid. (Italics added for emphasis.)

158 Ainsztein, op. cit., p. 271.

159 The first was the 1812 war against Napoleon.

160 Jewish Chronicle, July 4, 1942.

161 Jewish Chronicle, September 26, 1941.

162 Jewish Chronicle, October 10, 1941.

163 Jewish Chronicle, January 2, 1942.

164 Jewish Chronicle, October 17, 1941.

165 Shimon Redlich, unpublished manuscript, citing the Information Bulletin, Embassy of U.S.S.R., Washington, October 6, 1941. The Sovinformburo was the information department of the Ministry of Foreign Affairs.

166 American Jewish Year Book, 1942-1943 (New York and Philadelphia: The Jewish Publication Society of America, 1943, p. 238-239. This was part of Soviet propaganda.

167 This figure included statistics from the annexed territories in the West. Jewish Chronicle, August 29, 1941.

168 Judel Mark, "Jewish Schools in Soviet Russia," in Jacob Frumkin et al., eds., Russian Jewry 1917-1967 (New York: Thomas Yoseloff, 1969), p. 257.

169 Jewish Chronicle, July 11, 1941.

170 Jewish Chronicle, July 11, 1941, p. 1.

171 In the second instance, that of the recognition of the State of Israel, the interests of Soviet Jews were set apart.

172 J.T.A. (Jewish Telegraphic Agency), October 31, 1943.

173 The first was in April 1941, in Moscow. Among participants were delegates from Kiev and Minsk. Polish Jewish writers and editors attended the sessions, at which "the prestige enjoyed by Shlomo Mikhoels within the Soviet Jewish community was already apparent." Ch. Szmeruk, "Yiddish Publications in the U.S.S.R.," Yad Washem Studies, Vol. 4, Jerusalem, 1960, p, 111.

174 Yehoshua A. Gilboa, "Our Jewish Brethren the World Over," Bulletin on Soviet and East European Jewish Affairs, No. 5, May 1970, p. 78.

[175] Ehrenburg, op. cit., p. 107. (Emphasis added.)

[176] Jewish Chronicle, August 12, 1941.

[177] Jewish Chronicle, September 19, 1941.

[178] Jewish Chronicle, September 19, 1941.

[179] Cited in Calling All Jews to Action (London: Jewish Fund for Soviet Russia, 1943), p. 99.

[180] Ibid., p. 100.

[181] Goldberg, op. cit., p. 59.

[182] Gilboa, op. cit., p. 78.

[183] Schwarz, op. cit., p. 216.

[184] Ibid., p. 201. (S.M. Schwarz was one of the two Menshevik representatives in the Kerensky administration. He was chief of the Social Security Section, Department of Labor.)

[185] Ibid.

[186] Baron, op. cit., p. 304.

[187] Letter to writer, February 19, 1971. Interpolation by writer.

[188] Redlich, op. cit., p. 6.

[189] Ainsztein, op. cit., p. 283.

[190] See Appendix 1.

[191] Schwarz, op. cit., p. 202.

[192] Redlich, op. cit., p. 14.

[193] Schwarz, op. cit, p. 201.

[194] Jewish Chronicle , December 10, 1941.

[195] Gilboa, op, cit, p. 78.

[196] Schwarz, op. cit., p. 202.

[197] B.Z. Goldberg in a letter to writer, February 19, 1971.

[198] Solomon M. Schwarz, The Jews in the Soviet Union (Syracuse: Syracuse University Press, 1951), p. 216, note 23.

[199] Ilya Ehrenburg Memoirs 1921-1941 (New York: Grosset and Dunlap, 1966), p. 49A.

[200] Goldberg, in letter to writer, February 19, 1971.

[201] Ibid.

[202] Shimon Redlich, unpublished manuscript, p. 21.

[203] Ibid., p. 23.

[204] Ibid. , p. 72.

205 Redlich, op. cit. , p. 26; also Schwarz, op. cit. , p. 205.

206 Goldberg, op. cit., p. 62.

207 Ibid., p. 63.

208 Ibid.

209 Ibid., p. 61. (Emphasis added.)

210 A term used first in an announcement, on August 24, 1941, and subsequently for each of the public meetings held on the eve of the plenary sessions.

211 Jewish Chronicle, May 29, 1942.

212 Jewish Chronicle, May 29, 1942.

213 Redlich, op. cit., p. 28.

214 Schwarz, op. cit., p. 203.

215 Ibid.

216 Aynikayt, July 25, 1942.

217 Aynikayt, September 5, 1942.

218 Aynikayt, September 15, 1942

219 J.T.A., August 24, 1942.

220 Ibid.

221 An exception was a report of Shakno Epstein to the third plenary session of the J.A.C., in April 1944, which stated that "close to two million dollars were collected by Jewish organizations in the United States." (Aynikayt, April 13, 1944.)

222 Aynikayt, February 27, 1943.

223 The term "delegate" is not clear, in the sense there were no delegates representing areas, regions or groups. B.Z. Goldberg, was also puzzled by the distinction made between "representatives" and "delegates." From the study of the reports, it would appear that the term delegate was applied to people who attended regular work meetings.

224 Aynikayt, March 15, 1943.

225 Ibid., p. 4.

226 Ibid.

227 Ibid., p. 5.

228 Redlich, op. cit., p. 32.

229 Y.A. Gilboa, "Our Jewish Brethren the World Over," Bulletin on Soviet and East European Jewish Affairs, No. 7, May 1970, p. 81.

[230] Aynikayt, March 15, 1943, p. 5.

[231] Schwarz, op. cit., p. 202.

[232] Ibid., p. 205.

[233] Ch. Szmeruk, "Yiddish Publications in the U.S.S.R.," Yad Washem Studies, Vol. 4, Jerusalem, 1960, p. 121.

[234] Goldberg, op. cit., p. 47.

[235] Ibid., p. 47.

[236] Ibid., p. 46-47.

[237] Ibid., p. 144.

[238] Ibid.

[239] Ibid., p. 144.

[240] Ibid., p. 47.

[241] New York Times, July 9, 1943.

[242] J.T.A., October 25, 1943.

[243] J.T.A., October 31, 1943.

[244] Ibid.

[245] Jewish Chronicle, April 14, 1944.

[246] Goldberg, op. cit., p. 48.

[247] Ibid.

[248] Redlich, op. cit., p. 32.

[249] Jewish Chronicle, April 14, 1944.

[250] Ibid.

[251] Redlich, op, cit., p. 32.

[252] Szmeruk, op. cit., p. 121.

[253] Goldberg, op. cit., p. 61. (Underlined for emphasis.)

[254] S. L. Schneiderman, "Ilya Ehrenburg Reconsidered," Midstream, October 1968, p. 49.

[255] Aynikayt, August 24, 1944.

[256] Aynikayt, August 24, 1944.

[257] In a letter to writer, December 23, 1970.

[258] Goldberg interpreted the J.A.C.'s cooperation differently, when he observed: "The Moscow committee, cooperated whole-heartedly with the New York committee in assembling data." See Goldberg, op. cit., p. 61.

[259] Dr. M.L. Perlzweig was the leading official of the World Jewish Congress, and co-chairman of the New York Black Book Committee.

[260] Perlzweig's letter to writer, December 23, 1970.

[261] Goldberg, op. cit., p. 66.

[262] Letter to writer, December 23, 1970.

[263] Ibid.

[264] Ibid.

[265] Goldberg, op. cit., p. 65.

[266] Ibid., p. 66.

[267] Letter to writer, November 18, 1970.

[268] Unity in Dispersion, Institute of Jewish Affairs, New York, 1948.

[269] Letter to writer, December 23, 1970.

[270] S.L. Schneiderman, "Ehrenburg Reconsidered," Midstream, October 1968, p. 49.

[271] Goldberg, op. cit., p. 91.

[272] Szmeruk, op. cit., p. 121.

[273] Goldberg, op. cit., p. 121.

[274] Szmeruk, op. cit., p. 121.

[275] Goldberg, op. cit., p. 64.

[276] Ibid.

[277] Szmeruk, op. cit., p. 163.

[278] Aynikayt, February 7, 1943.

[279] Aynikayt, February 7, 1943.

[280] Szmeruk, op. cit., pp. 24-29.

[281] Ibid.

[282] Goldberg, op. cit., p. 97.

[283] Writer's letter from Moscow to the World Jewish Congress, in London, January 13, 1945 (Central Zionist Archives, Jerusalem.)

[284] Redlich, op. cit., op. 40.

[285] Goldberg, op. cit., p. 59.

[286] Frantisek Nemec and Vladimir Moudry, Soviet Seizure of Subcarpathian Ruthenia (Toronto: William B. Anderson, 1955), p. 63-64.

[287] Hereafter referred to as W.J.C.

[288] Jewish Chronicle, November 19, 1944.

[289] See text of official press release, Jewish Chronicle, November 19, 1944.

[290] Told to me by an official of the J.A.C.

[291] We conducted all our conversations in the English language. Epstein had allegedly lived in the United States as an agent of the Soviet secret service.

[292] J.T.A., October 31, 1943.

[293] J.T.A., October 25, 1943.

[294] Copy of telegram in (Central Zionist Archives, Jerusalem.)

[295] Letter from the Czechoslovak Ministry of Foreign Affairs, December 18, 1944 (Central Zionist Archives(Jerusalem.)

[296] Also, the fact that an American, Rabbi Stephen S. Wise, was not only the leader of the American Jewish Congress, but also one of the founding members of the W.J.C.

[297] It will be recalled that in 1943, Fefer, himself, stated in New York: "The Jews in the Soviet Union and in the United States are the majority of the Jewish people. Together we are ten million Jews. Upon us lies the responsibility for the fate of the Jewish people." (See footnote 45, Chapter VI.)

[298] Letter to writer, February 26, 1945, (file A280/25 Central Zionist Archives, Jerusalem.)

[299] M.L. Perlzweig to writer, December 23, 1970.

[300] Ben Zion Goldberg, The Jewish Problem in the Soviet Union (New York: Crown Publication Inc., 1961), p. 59.

[301] Ibid., p. 59.

[302] Goldberg is the son-in-law of Sholom Alechem.

[303] Goldberg, op. cit., p. 67.

[304] Ibid., P. 80.

[305] Perlzweig's letter to author, December 22, 1970.

[306] Arthur Schlessinger, Jr., "Origins of the Cold War," Foreign Affairs, vol. 46, October 1967, pp. 23-52.

[307] Ibid., p. 44.

[308] B.Z. Goldberg The Jewish Problem in the Soviet Union (New York: Crown Publications Inc., 1961, p. 100.

[309] Ibid., p. 202.

[310] Ibid., p. 99.

[311] Schlessinger, op. cit., p. 45.

[312] Ibid., p. 51.

[313] Ibid.

[314] Ibid., p. 52.

[315] Ch. Szmeruk, "Yiddish Publications in the U.S.S.R.," Yad Washem Studies, vol. 47 Jerusalem, 1960, p. 264.

[316] S. Redlich, untitled manuscript (New York: Academic Committee on Soviet Jewry [n. d. 3), p. 63.

[317] S.L. Schneiderman, "Ilya Ehrenburg Reconsidered," Midstream, October 1968, p. 53.

[318] Ibid.

[319] Goldberg, op. cit., pp. 100-101.

[320] Schneiderman, op. cit., p, 49.

[321] Goldberg, op cit., p. 141.

[322] Schneiderman, op. cit., p. 53.

[323] Ibid., p. 53.

[324] Goldberg, op. cit., p. 141. Years later, N. Krushchev told the former Canadian Communist, J. B. Salsberg, that "he agreed with Stalin's opinion that the Crimea should not be made into a centre of a Jewish settlement, since in case of war it could form a bridgehead against the U.S.S.R." Ibid., p. 148.

[325] Schneiderman, op. cit., p. 53.

[326] Ibid.

[327] Goldberg, op. cit., p. 141.

[328] The American Joint Jewish Distribution Committee, a social welfare organization, operating for more than a half a century in many countries of the world.

[329] For example, the trial of Rudolf Slansky and his associates.

[330] Goldberg, op. cit., p. 104.

[331] Ibid.

[332] Ibid., p. 101.

[333] Schneiderman, op. cit., p. 53.

[334] Goldberg, op. cit., p. 68.

[335] The verification of the date of execution was secured by Leon Crystal, United Nations reporter for the Jewish Daily Forward. The news was corroborated, semiofficially in the Communist Yiddish daily Folkshtime in Warsaw. (Goldberg, op. cit., p. 113.)

[336] Esther Rosenthal-Schneiderman, "Jewish Communists in the U.S.S.R., 1926-1958," Bulletin on Soviet and East European Jewish Affairs, No. 5, May 1970, p. 57.

[337] Solomon M. Schwarz, The Jews in the Soviet Union (Syracuse: Syracuse University Press, 1951), p. 216.

BIBLIOGRAPHY

BOOKS AND THESES

Ainsztein, Reuben. "Soviet Jewry in the Second World War." in L. Kochan (ed..), *The Jews in Soviet Russia since 1917.* London: Oxford University Press, 1970.

Alliluyeva, Svetlana. *Only One Year.* New York: Harper and Row, 1969.

American Jewish Year Book, 1942-1943. New York and Philadelphia: Jewish Publication Society of America, 1943.

Aronson, Gregor. "The Jewish Question in the Stalin Era," in Jacob Frumkin *et al.* (eds.). *Russian Jewry 1917-1967.* New York: Thomas Yoseloff, 1969.

Barghorn, Frederick C. *Soviet Russian Nationalism.* New York: Oxford University Press, 1956.

Baron, Salo W. *The Russian Jew Under Tsars and Soviets.* New York: The Macmillan Company, 1964.

Bottomore, T.B. (ed.). *Karl Marx, Early Writings.* New York: McGraw-Hill Book Company, 1963.

Buber-Neumann, M. *Mistress to Kafka.* London: Seeker and Warburg Ltd., 1966.

Cang, Joel. *The Silent Millions: a history of the Jews in the Soviet Union.* London: Rapp and Whitting, 1969.

Cohen, Israel. *Contemporary Jewry.* London: Metheun & Co. Ltd., 1950.

Conquest, Robert (ed.). *Soviet Nationalities Policy in Practice.* London: The Bodley Read Ltd., 1967.

The Politics of Ideas in U.S.S.R. New York: Frederick A. Praeger, 1967.

Deutscher, Isaac. *The Non-Jewish Jew and Other Essays.* New York: Oxford University Press. 1968.

Dubnov, S.M. *History of Jews in Russia and Poland.* Vol. 3. Philadelphia: The Jewish Publication Society of America, 1920.

Nationalism and History. Cleveland: Meridan Books and The Jewish Publication Society, 1961.

Ehrenburg, Ilya. *Memoirs 1921-1941.* New York: Grosset and Dunlap, 1966

Epstein, Melech. *The Jew and Communism.* New York: Trade Union Sponsoring Committee, 1959.

Esh, Shaul (ed.). *Yad Washem Studies on the European Jewish Catastrophe and Resistance.* Vol. IV. Jerusalem: Yad Washem, 1960.

Ettinger, S. "The Jews in Russia at the Outbreak of the Revolution," in L. Kochan (ed.), *The Jews in Soviet Russia since 1917*. London: Oxford University Press, 1970.

Fainsod, Merle. *Smolensk Under Soviet Rule*. New York: Vintage Books, 1963.

Getzler, Israel. *Martov: a Political Biography of a Russian Social Democrat*. Cambridge: Cambridge University Press, 1967.

Gitelman, Z.Y. "The Jewish Sections of the Communist Party and the Modernization of Soviet Jewry," unpublished Ph.D. thesis. New York: Columbia University, 1968, microfilm.

Goldberg, Ben Zion. *The Jewish Problem in the Soviet Union*. New York: Crown Publication Inc., 1961.

Goldman, Guido G. *Zionism Under Soviet Rule*. New York: Herzl Press, 1960.

Greenberg, Louis. *The Jews in Russia*. New Haven and London: Yale University Press, 1965.

Hilberg, Raoul. *The Destruction of European Jews*. Chicago: Quadrangle Books, 1961.

Janovsky, Oscar. *The Jews and Minority Rights*. New York: Columbia University Press, 1933.

Korey, William. "The Legal Position of Soviet Jewry," in L. Kochan (ed.). *The Jews in Soviet Russia since 1917*. London: Oxford University Press, 1970.

Lamont, Corliss. *The Peoples of the Soviet Union*. New York: Harcourt, Brace and Company, 1944.

Lawrence, Gunther. *Three Million More?* New York: Doubleday, 1970.

Leibler, Isi. *Soviet Jewry and Human Rights*. Melbourne: Ramsay, Ware Publishing PTY. Ltd., 1965.

Lenin on the Jewish Question. New York: New York International Publishers Co. Inc., 1934.

Levin, Shmarya. *Forward from Exile*. Philadelphia: The Jewish Publication Society of America, 1967.

Mark, Judel. "Jewish Schools in Soviet Russia," in Jacob Frumkin *et al.(eds.)*, *Russian Jewry 1917-1967*. New York: Thomas Yoseloff, 1969.

Masaryk, T.G. *The Spirit of Russia*, 2 vols. London: George Allen and Unwin, 1961.

Miller, Jacob. "Soviet Theory on Jews," in L. Kochan (ed.). *The Jews in Soviet Russia since 1917*. London: Oxford University Press, 1970.

Moudry, Vladimir; Frantisek, Nemec. *Soviet Seizure of Subcarpatian Ruthenia.* Toronto: William B. Anderson, 1955.

Nove, Alex; Newth, T.A. "The Jewish Population: Demographis Jews and Occupational Patterns," in L. Kochan (ed.). *The Jews in Soviet Russia since 1917.* London: Oxford University Press, 1970.

Novick, Paul. Jews in the Soviet Union New York: Morning Freiheit, 1965.

Pipes, Richard. *The Formation of the Soviet Union, Communism and Nationalism 1917-1923.* Cambridge: Harvard University Press, 1964.

Rabinovich, Solomon. *Jews in the Soviet Union.* Moscow: Novosti Press Agency Publishing House, 1965.

Rabinovicz, Harry M. *The Legacy of Polish Jewry.* London: Thomas Yoseloff, 1965.

Redlich, Shimon. *Untitled Manuscript on the Jewish Anti-Fascist Committee.* New York: Academic Committee on Soviet Jewry (n.d.).

Rosenthal, Herman. "Russia," *The Jewish Encyclopedia,* Vol. 10. New York: Funk and Wagnalls Co., 1905, pp. 518-519.

Rothenberg, Joshua. "Jewish Religion in the Soviet Union," in L. Kochan (ed.), *The Jews in Soviet Russia since 1917.* . London: Oxford University Press, 1970.

Rubin, Ronald I. *The Unredeemed.* Chicago: Quadrangle Books, 1968.

Schechtman, Joseph B. *Star in Eclipse, Russian Jewry Revisited.* New York: Thomas Yoseloff, 1961.

_____. "The USSR, Zionism and Israel," in L. Kochan (ed.), *The Jews in Soviet Russia since 1917.* London: Oxford University Press, 1970.

Schwarz, Solomon M. *The Jews in the Soviet Union.* Syracuse: University Press, 1951.

_____. "Birobidzhan," in Jacob Frumkin et al. (eds.), *Russian Jewry 1917-1967.* New York: Thomas Yoseloff, 1969.

Shaheen, Samall. *The Communist (Bolshevik) Theory of National Self-Determination.* The Hague: W. Van Hoeve Ltd., 1956.

Stein, Leonard. *The Letters and Papers of Chaim Weizman.* Vol. 1. London: Oxford University Press, 1968.

Teller, Judd L. *The Kremlin, the Jews and the Middle East.* New York: Thomas Yoseloff, 1957.

Tsamerian, I.P.; Ronin, S.L. *Equality of Rights Between Races and Nationalities in the U.S.S.R.* Paris: Unesco, 1962.

West, Benjamin. *Struggles of a Generation.* Tel Aviv: Massada Publishing Co., 1959.

ARTICLES

Budish, I.M. "Birobidzhan," The American Review on the Soviet Union. Vol. IX, 1948.

Decter, Moshe. "The Status of Jews in the Soviet Union," Foreign Affairs, Vol. 41, No. 2, January 1963.

Friedberg, Maurice, "The State of Soviet Jewry," Commentary, Vol. 39, No. 1, 1968.

Gilboa, Jehoshua A. "Our Jewish Brethren the World Over," Bulletin on Soviet and East European Jewish Affairs, No. 5, May 1970.

Harcave, Sidney. "The Jews and the First Russian National Election," The American Slavic and East European Review, Vol. 9, 1950.

Levenberg, S. "The Soviet Union and the Jewish Problem," Calling All Jews to Action. London: Jewish Fund for Soviet Russia, 1943.

Rosenthal Schneiderman, Esther. "Jewish Communists in the USSR, 1926-1958," Bulletin on Soviet and East European Jewish Affairs, No. 5, 1970.

Schlesinger, Arthur, Jr. "Origins of the Cold War," Foreign Affairs, Vol. 46, October 1967.

Schneiderman, S.L. "Ilya Ehrenburg reconsidered," Midstream, October 1968.

Szmeruk, Ch. "Yiddish Publications in the U.S.S.R.," Yad Washem Studies, Vol. 4, Jerusalem, 1960.

"Verblibene Dokumenten fin Erlich un Alter," (Yiddish), Unser Tsait, Vol. 7, July 1943.

PERIODICALS

Aynikayt, Moscow, Organ of the Jewish Anti-Fascist Committee in the USSR, from June 1942 to November 1948.

Jewish Chronicle, London, 1941-1944.

Jewish Telegraphic Agency, London, 1943.

New York Times, New York, July 1943.

ARCHIVES

Dr. Lev Zelmanovits Papers, A280/25, (Central Zionist Archives, Jerusalem.)

REPORTS

Rosenberg, I. Report to the Administrative Committee of the World Jewish Congress, New York: February 15, 1946. Mimeo.

Rosenberg, I. *Report of the British Section of the World Jewish Congress*, London, July 3, 1945.

Unity in Dispersion, Institute of Jewish Affairs, New York, 1948.

CORRESPONDENCE

Abramowitz, Dina, Librarian, Yivo Institute for Jewish Research, New York, December 24, 1970.

Eppler, Elisabeth E., Librarian, Institute of Jewish Affairs, London, December 29, 1970.

Goldberg, Ben Zion, editor The Day, New York, February 19, 1971.

Perlzweig, Maurice L., Director General, World Jewish Congress, New York, December 22, 23, 1970.

PART II

COREY GOLDMAN

A PORTRAIT OF IMRE YITZHAK ROSENBERG

CHAPTER I

THE BIAS OF HUMAN NATURE

There are many stories told about the events during the Second World War and particularly during Hitler's campaign to annihilate the Jews. Despite all the atrocities of war itself and the systematic killing of Europe's Jews and other ethnic and social groups, millions upon millions of individual stories have occurred and probably never will be told.

Steven Spielberg has made a valiant attempt to break down the bias and record the stories of all survivors. Through the Shoah Foundation, more than one million survivors have had the opportunity to share their tales and have them digitally archived for eternity. The Shoah Foundation was a massive step forward in documenting the atrocities of the Second World War. However, the precise stories of those survivors will never be told because of the elements of time or of individual perception and interpretation. From a philosophical point of view, the argument is simple: no two people can ever tell the same story exactly the same way.

Such is the story of Imrich (Imre) Yitzhak Rosenberg and the rescue and flight of 301 orphan children from Theresienstadt[1] concentration camp at the end of the Second World War. Like thousands of others, Imre's story never made it into the historical mainstream. His name is not affiliated with the complicated effort surrounding the unusual rescue. Organizations such as the '45 Aid Society, whose members comprise the rescued Theresienstadt children, and Yad Vashem, one of the more revered institutions that has painstakingly documented the Holocaust, have yet to officially acknowledge Rosenberg's involvement in the rescue, despite his own historical records that prove it. In Yad Vashem's case, the current historical record indicates that "fewer than 100" orphaned children remained when Theresienstadt was liberated. Rosenberg's own records, as well as records obtained from the British and Czech governments, emphatically correct that number to 301.

Why is it that a man's gallant efforts to help others during the Second World War, particularly in ways that by most standards were above and beyond the call of duty, were largely ignored and shunned by the mainstream? Even after the subject himself presented his own historical facts and testimony to confirm his own involvement, why was the historical record not changed to reflect his heroic achievement? The answer probably lies with human nature. The positive aspect of that kind of due diligence is the existence of a standard — a set of rules and guidelines that ensures appropriate selection takes place before an event becomes part of the historical record. The negative aspect, unfortunately, is the politics and wrangling that typically occur between individuals and institutions that, for reasons of personal and / or collective interest, are often more driven by recognition and philanthropy than by an ever-present drive to constantly adjust, clarify and enhance the fuzzy picture of the past.

Of course, it is not just Rosenberg's story that has never made it to the official historical record. The tales of many individuals who made liberation possible and arranged for those Jews who remained after the Second World War to be moved out of concentration camps back to their home towns in Central Europe or to North America or elsewhere, have escaped pen and paper. In some cases, it's because their stories have simply been overlooked or because historians didn't deem their stories worth telling to a general audience. In still others, heroic acts during and after the Second World War have never been documented for the simple reason that those individuals never thought it necessary to advertise their heroism.

This story is about one such individual.

CHAPTER II

THE STORY BEGINS

Imre Yitzhak Rosenberg wasn't a particularly imposing man. He was of average height, with a medium build and dark hair that he always combed straight back. He was always dressed impeccably, wearing classic, tailored clothes constructed of good fabrics and sewn by proper tailors. His social status wasn't particularly important to him, but he was a man interested in politics, social causes and the general good of humanity.

Born in 1913, he was one of two children of a Jewish family from Nove Mesto Nad Vahom, a medium-sized town in the northern region of what is presently Slovakia in Central Europe. His father owned and operated a shop that provided hand-made home and office furnishings. He was a quiet, unassuming young man who was as interested in books and art as he was in sports and social activities. Early in his life, he was a typical child, typical teenager and a typical young man. Later on, he was a solid devoted husband, scholar, painter and steadfast member of the Ottawa Jewish community. He wasn't, on the surface, an extraordinary individual. Yet, he lived an extraordinary life, helping hundreds directly and thousands indirectly escape death during the Second World War and the Holocaust, and to rebuild their lives in its aftermath.

It wasn't until near the end of his life that he decided to tell his real story. By then he was living in Ottawa, Canada, retired from his successful real estate practice and from his part-time work as a professor of political science at St. Patrick's College, which later became part of Carleton University. He chose to tell his own story after committing himself to listening to so many others. Rosenberg also spent much of his time in Ottawa as a private member of the Refugee Status Advisory Committee on behalf of the federal government, which worked to make it easier for refugees to enter Canada and establish themselves within its borders.

Like thousands of other refugees fleeing their homeland in disarray, Rosenberg arrived in Canada shortly after the Second World War in the spring of 1949. He had little money, no immediate family and no one to turn to for help. The government he had so diligently served was no longer in power. His former homeland, Czechoslovakia, was in a postwar state of political and social turmoil, thanks to the questionable death of Foreign Affairs Minister Jan Masaryk, with whom Rosenberg worked closely. The new Communist government had confiscated his home and belongings. His family was gone. His history was gone. He had nowhere to go.

When he arrived in Canada, Rosenberg first attempted to attach himself to the Jewish community. He needed shelter and a job. Unfamiliar with the social milieu of Ottawa's small Jewish collective, he contacted various individuals who offered him nothing.

Rosenberg quickly joined his friend Frantisek Nemec, former Czech ambassador to Canada, and his wife, working in a small tea room in Ottawa's market district. The three exiled friends helped run the small tea room. Mr. and Mrs. Nemec both cooked and served the customers, while Imre cleaned the tables and washed the dishes. Nemec, who had sponsored Rosenberg's entry to Canada as a landed immigrant, was Rosenberg's link to his old life and helped him to make a fresh start in a country where he was not being wrongly hunted for treason and conspiracy. The job's meagre salary allowed him to rent a one-room flat above the store with little spare change for food or much else. It didn't matter much to Rosenberg, as the job and the room were only a place to start.

With a career beyond dishwashing in mind, and with his legal and political education and experience, it seemed natural for Rosenberg to turn to the Canadian government for a job. As a high-ranking official in the former Czechoslovak government with a Doctorate in Law and postgraduate studies at The Hague School of International Law, he was more than qualified to handle any one of dozens of positions in government, particularly with his specialized training in international relations and immigration law.

Unfortunately, few in the Canadian government saw Rosenberg's qualifications in the same way. He kept the stack of rejection letters in a small file among his memoirs, as a reminder of how he could never return to the life he once had. His days as a government attaché were over.

He never publicly complained about the way he was received in Canada after his notable, albeit short, career as a diplomat for the Czechoslovak government during and after the Second World War. He knew he was in a country that judged his accent more than his credentials and that viewed his education and experience as being unimportant. Even though he spoke five languages, held two degrees and had enough work experience to make some of the more senior officials within the Canadian government blush, he knew he would never receive proper credit.

Maybe that explains why he chose to bury his colourful past and work so diligently to create a new life for himself in Canada as a businessman, teacher, husband and painter. Perhaps it also explains why he chose to wait almost forty years to correct the historical record that to this day lists events during and after the Second World War that he was clearly involved in without mention of his name.

Rosenberg died at the wheel of his car on June 26, 1986. Just before he left his office, he methodically cleared his desk of the collection of papers and research he had assembled to begin writing his autobiography. Rosenberg's autobiography was to include the testimony of his involvement in the transfer of 301 orphan children from the Theresienstadt concentration camp in Czechoslovakia to England at the end of the Second World War. It was also to include many other events and memoirs that are currently either not documented or are recorded incorrectly, including Rosenberg's involvement in the exiled Czechoslovak government and his passionate allegiance to both the government and country he served and to the people he belonged — the Jewish people.

This story is about an individual who never wanted to be recognized as a man of charity. This is a story about an individual who took pleasure in helping others gain dignity, respect and decency for themselves and, in turn, use that to make the world a better place. This is a story that Rosenberg, in all likelihood would not have wanted told in such detail. This is the story of Imre Yitzhak Rosenberg, who would never have defined himself a hero.

CHAPTER III

WHAT MAKES A HERO?

Hero, as defined by the Oxford dictionary, is "A man distinguished by extraordinary valour, firmness, fortitude, or greatness of soul; a man admired and venerated for his achievements and noble qualities, a warrior." Folklore suggests a hero is a selfless individual who has a passionate commitment to helping those less fortunate. A true hero doesn't act out of self-interest; he places his own interests and objectives in the background for the sole purpose of helping others. Rosenberg was such a man. He spent much of his life devoted to helping others, almost always putting himself second to their needs, no matter how small.

Why is it that society feels the need to classify people who have done good for others in a special way with a special word or phrase? Whether they are simple acts of kindness or generosity or tasks of compassion and bravery, millions of individuals do good things for each other every day and are not recognized for it. In many cases, the reason they aren't recognized is that those people make a conscious choice to make their actions anonymous. In other cases, it's because society, in its relentless effort to define what a "hero" is, dismisses what it sees as ordinary, commonplace tasks as unworthy of special attention. Rosenberg fell under both categories. His efforts to help people during and after the Second World War were nothing short of gallant, yet he chose not to have those efforts recognized until the inaccuracy of the public record of those same events tore into his conscience and forced him to action.

Some of the other events in his life include his undying devotion to having what's known as The Precious Legacy Exhibit (a collection of artifacts stolen from Jewish families who perished in the Second World War) removed from the Czech Republic and transported for public showing in other countries. He also worked on the federal Refugee Committee in Ottawa, responsible for opening Canada's doors to individuals fleeing persecution from other countries. His story is the tale of all people who perform gallant and unselfish acts to make the world a better place, and despite their efforts and love for humanity have never been defined as heroes.

The early years of Rosenberg's life weren't much different from any other young Jewish boy growing up in Central Europe during the 1920s. The First World War ended at the same time Rosenberg began public school. When he was 15, he joined a group called *Hashomer*, which is a Jewish youth movement similar to the Boy Scouts. A year later he established an organization called El Al, which was a national Zionist high school students' association, where he acted as the chairman. Throughout the late 1920s and early 1930s, Rosenberg was extremely active in Jewish and Zionist causes. Through *El Al*, he organized the first Zionist summer camp for Jewish children. At the same time, he became editor of a weekly Jewish newspaper called *Hamaccabi*. He also wrote for several other Jewish publications, including *Zidovske Zpravy*, a Czech language weekly, *Zidovske Noviny*, a Slovak language biweekly and *Selbstwehr* and a German-Jewish weekly. He was proficient in all three languages, as well as Russian and English.

Rosenberg continued with his pro-Jewish efforts after graduation from Stefanikov High School in 1931. He was elected to the national executive of Maccabi Hatzair — a Zionist organization involved in developing Palestine as a Jewish homeland. At the same time, he became secretary-general to the president of the Parliamentary Jewish Party in Czechoslovakia — his first government appointment.

Even though he had deep roots in the Jewish community, Rosenberg realized from an early age that it was important to maintain ties outside the Jewish community, and to further his education in the secular world. His activities were not tied solely to the community that surrounded him. His studies in law, with primary interest in minorities and constitutional issues, gave him a basis for knowledge and action in dealing with human rights in general and Jewish needs in particular.

Rosenberg did not toss away his ties to the Jewish community in which he was raised, as his connection with Zionism and Judaism, which began early in his life, remained strong. Similar to many other young Jews living in Europe at the time, he developed an equal sense of nationalism to both his country of birth and to the region of what would eventually become the Jewish homeland.

In 1933, a year after he began studying law at Komensky University, Rosenberg travelled to Palestine. He saw and admired the efforts of Jews who had chosen to leave the modernity and prosperity of Europe behind them to build a home in Palestine. He travelled throughout the underdeveloped country, taking in its sights, sounds and history. He helped found and build Kfar Hammacabi, one of the first kibbutzim in Palestine. He admired the vitality and perseverance of Jews willing to sacrifice the comforts of modern Europe to build a homeland for their people, even though many other Jews around the world saw their efforts as unnecessary and somewhat in vain. Rosenberg's trip to Palestine was the genesis of his decision to involve himself in Jewish causes. Zionism, Judaism and the success of both became an intrinsic part of his life.

"It was beautiful," he scribbled on the back of a scrap piece of paper en route back to Czechoslovakia following his first visit. "The land was beautiful, the people were beautiful, the air and sky more clear and beautiful than I'd ever seen. They were dirty, sweaty, tired, but with such energy as I'd never seen before. This was their home."[2]

Rosenberg returned to Czechoslovakia now more determined than ever to be a part of the growing Zionist movement, and to support Palestine as a Jewish homeland. In 1933, he volunteered to be the personal assistant of Dr. Oskar Neuman of the Jewish National Fund, which raised money to help Jews settle in Palestine. He also became a member of the Hanhala Olamith (a Zionist organization based in Berlin), which later merged with several other European Zionist causes to become Ichud Hakvutzot V'Kibbutzim (a Zionist group that urged resettlement of Jews to kibbutzim in Palestine).

For the next six years, Rosenberg found himself increasingly involved in all kinds of Jewish activities. Not unlike thousands of other Jews and non-Jews in the prewar period, Rosenberg fought against what he thought was wrong, committing himself to what was right. He was young, educated, and painfully aware of the turmoil Europe was about to enter; for him it seemed natural to be as involved as possible in as many different ways of trying to prevent that turmoil from erupting. By March 1939, Rosenberg was conscious that it was pointless to try to prevent Adolph Hitler's Nazis from taking over Eastern and Central Europe, trying to dissuade people from being swept up in its ideology. With Europe just months away from war, he decided to focus all his attention on getting as many Jews away from Hitler's clutches as possible.

"I knew what was in store for the Jews of Europe," he later wrote in his memoirs. "I didn't know exactly how or when, but I knew of their demise. I also knew I had to work on convincing as many Jews as I could that they weren't safe, and I had to work to guide them safely away to Palestine or anywhere else they were still permitted to go at that time."[3]

Under the authority and guidance of the then-Slovak government, Rosenberg travelled to London, where he established a secretariat within the offices of the Maccabi World Union. From there, he arranged to help Jewish families leave Europe for a safer environment. He returned to the eastern part of Slovakia, where he negotiated with government officials to allow him to travel freely throughout the country to "promote emigration to Palestine" in the hope of saving Jews from what he felt would be imminent persecution. He posted signs in schools, community centres, at tram stops and in restaurants, offering to help any Jewish family wanting to leave the country. The response was less than overwhelming. Fewer than 100 families took him up on his offer, despite Germany's disdainful view of the Jewish people and of the growing problem of anti-Semitism in Central and Western Europe. Some 8,000 other families remained behind.

From the time he was eighteen, Rosenberg focused his life and his career on helping others that found themselves in the wrong place at one of the worst times in human history. Partly by fate, partly by purpose and mostly be sheer luck, Rosenberg was able to save the lives of many individuals who otherwise wouldn't have had the opportunity, the position or the strength to do it themselves.

And so it happened that much of what a man named Imre Yitzhak Rosenberg had managed to accomplish early in his life, would be reflected in one mission that would save the lives of hundreds, if not thousands of people. Through his unwavering commitment to Judaism and the Jewish people, and through his equal commitment to his government and his country, Rosenberg would manage to orchestrate one of the most unusual missions of hope arranged in the aftermath of the Second World War and the Holocaust. It is a story that must be told because Rosenberg died shortly after he finally decided to clear up the inaccuracies surrounding the story.

CHAPTER IV

A JEW IN DEED

In January 1939, armed with a recent law degree, Rosenberg made his way to Holland to specialize in international law in The Hague. His attendance at school was sporadic, since Rosenberg opted to spend much of his time on extracurricular activities, namely, helping organize rescue efforts of European Jews, stripped of their citizenship and increasingly under political and social attack, from widespread and growing anti-Semitism. With the help of a few friends working as clerks in the British government's birth certificate and registration office, Rosenberg was able to supply a number of false student certificates to his colleagues.

"A gentleman by the name of Lord Melchett, whom I met at a university function in The Hague, helped me arrange the whole thing, mostly the funding," Rosenberg wrote to his parents in Nove Mesto, in 1939. "He seems as fascinated and concerned with the future of Jews in Europe as I am, which is a rare commodity in such a society that turns more unusual by the day." [4]

Propelled by a desire to become increasingly involved in Jewish causes, Rosenberg travelled to Palestine for the second time, in the summer of 1939. With his law degree, a few dollars in his pocket and an even fewer number of personal belongings, Rosenberg visited Kfar Hamaccabi for a second time — this time to attend a Maccabi Hatzair convention.

The purpose of this mission was to assemble Jewish leaders, who were North American and European, as well as other interested parties. They would develop a concrete plan to warn the Jews of Europe about their fate if and when Hitler initiated the Second World War, and his program to annihilate the Jewish people.

By this time, many European and American Jewish organizations were mobilizing their efforts for three reasons. The first was to ensure the safety and security of Europe's Jews. Since most Jews at the time had lost their rights as citizens, groups such as Maccabi Hatzair, the World Jewish Congress and others, began a global lobbying campaign to encourage governments and other organizations to fight the mistreatment of Jews.

The second reason was to establish a grand-scale public relations campaign to convince Europe's Jews that Hitler's vision of a greater Germany didn't include them. Representatives from Germany, Russia, Poland, Austria, France, Britain and Belgium all attended the conference in Jerusalem to discuss the best way to get the message out to their people.

The third and most important objective of the delegates was to arrange for the emigration of Jews from Poland, Austria and Czechoslovakia to other regions of the world, mostly to Palestine. To do this, Rosenberg knew he'd require the support of the various European governments to allow himself and others to remove Jews from their country. There wasn't a problem with requesting that the Jews be removed from Central Europe, as most of Europe's leaders were more than willing to see them relocated somewhere else. The problem for Rosenberg, as a Jew, was to convince officials that the Jews could be persuaded to leave Central Europe of their own free will, and that their departure could be organized in a political-friendly manner, without causing negative international attention.

"I was faced with a dilemma," Rosenberg wrote in his memoirs. "I wasn't a Communist. I had never been a Communist, and I never would be one. With the takeover of the Slovak half of the country by Hlinka's fascist party under the leadership of Jozef Tiso, I had to make a choice. Either I could stubbornly refuse to recognize the take over of Slovakia by a government sympathetic to Germany and its chancellor, or I could accept the situation and use it to my advantage to help others. I chose the latter." [5]

The period leading up to the Second World War was an unprecedented time in the history of the human race. Families were torn apart and displaced, jobs lost, fortunes wiped out and political and monetary power transferred at an unparalleled pace.

To cope with the times, many people adapted themselves in various ways to these changes. Many Germans, for example, embraced Hitler's Nazi regime, even though most people neither voted for nor condoned his rise to power. Poles, Czechs and other nationalities embraced Hitler's annexation of their country on the surface for the simple reason they had little choice but to do so. In order to live a normal existence in prewar Europe, it can be argued that one had to join the majority or suffer the consequences. Rosenberg wasn't any different than the millions of other people who accepted change and adapted to it in order to accomplish their objectives.

In March 1938, through a series of orchestrated moves initiated by the German government to make the existing government of Czechoslovakia appear incompetent, Hitler seized power. Almost overnight, the democracy of Czechoslovakia became a puppet regime and an extension of the Third Reich. The Allied powers did little to stop the takeover. Only Russia refused to recognize the situation in Central Europe.

In light of these events, Rosenberg found himself faced with a choice. Either he could publicly declare himself against the German-aligned government, which he clearly was, or he could swallow his pride, accept the situation and use it to his advantage and to the advantage of others.

When Rosenberg attended the conference in Israel in the summer of 1939 on organizing the safe and effective removal of Jews from the now-occupied region of Czechoslovakia, he went as a supporter of the fascist regime now in control of his country of birth. He went under the guise of a Communist supporter under the personal approbation of President Jozef Tiso. That decision was probably the turning point in Rosenberg's career, helping him later to move seamlessly between his position with the Allied forces, and at the same time through some of the less friendly regions of Europe with little difficulty. This was a rarity for any individual, never mind a Jew, during the Second World War.

For most of that year, Rosenberg travelled from city to city across Europe, attending conferences, meetings and rallies in support of saving the Jews. He went to London to enlist as a volunteer with the

British chapter of the Jewish Agency, which was an organization based in Palestine that specialized in helping Jews emigrate to the region. He became secretary to Selig Brodetsky, then chairman of the Maccabi World Union. While in London, Rosenberg also took over the Maccabi Self-Help Association, which offered financial assistance and advice to Jewish refugees. Rosenberg then went to Geneva, where he participated in the last Zionist Congressional meeting before the outbreak of the Second World War.

Unlike many governments that were forced to step aside after being annexed by Hitler's government, the Czechoslovak government under the leadership of President Eduard Benes was sympathetic to the plight of the Jews. While Benes had publicly dissolved the Czechoslovak parliament and resigned as leader of the country in 1938, he still maintained his authority as President, and he worked hard to gain the support of other exiled Czechs. To be sure, the crux of his support came from the bourgeois who fled Nazi-occupied Czechoslovakia after 1938. In 1939, Benes and his supporters established the National Committee in France and began organizing military units among the Czechoslovak citizens who had fled and those that had settled abroad. Their goal, in line with the objective of the allied governments of England and France at the time, was to drive Germany into war with Russia, causing both powers to weaken each other and averting war on a much grander scale. Needless to say, the plan failed. After the fall of France to the Germans in 1940, Benes and his supporters moved to England and officially set up what became known as the Czechoslovak provisional government, or government in exile. In whatever capacity he could, Benes ruled his government-in-exile with as much autonomy as he could manage.

Through fate, circumstance, or luck, Rosenberg found himself in London on the eve of the Second World War. Fate, because it put him in the same place as the Czechoslovak government in exile, which was a government he supported and which supported him. Circumstance, because he was on his way back to Czechoslovakia at the time, and happened to find himself in a country against, rather than for, Hitler. And luck, because he really had no specific plan to be in London at the time.

While Rosenberg had no intention of returning to his homeland, he still found it difficult to accept that he couldn't return to his parents or family if he wanted to. Rather than dwell on his misfortunes, Rosenberg chose to do something about it. He joined the First Czechoslovak Brigade in England, which was the same army President Benes had orchestrated to handle the repatriation of his country. And so it happened that Rosenberg became involved with the Czechoslovak government-in-exile and its officials, first in Prague and later in London.

When Rosenberg joined the brigade in the early months of 1940, he planned to participate as a Jew, working with other Jews to help defend Jews and other civilians caught in the crossfire of war. It didn't quite turn out that way.

Although Rosenberg never concealed his Jewish identity during his time of service to President Benes and the Czechoslovak government-in-exile, his profile was that of a diplomat. Most Jews living under German control had been stripped of their legal rights. They had no income and no claim to property or possessions. They were forced to wear yellow stars on their clothes to identify themselves as Jews. Their only form of livelihood, in the loosest sense of the word, were the newly built detainment camps throughout Central Europe, where they worked as slave labourers.

Without doubt, Rosenberg's position was highly unusual. Few other Jews were involved in any senior government position within any government in 1939, particularly one based in Central Europe. As enlightened as the Benes government was, Jews were not considered on an equal social footing in politics. Jews looked after their own towns and communities but rarely, if it all, represented society at large in any capacity.

Rosenberg was fortunate enough to be in the right place at the right time, and he quickly moved up the political ladder in the Benes government in England, elevating himself to positions of authority. He first worked as a clerk on behalf of the information section of the Czechoslovak Ministry of Foreign Affairs, and later as a legal representative for the Ministry of Public Works and Agriculture. Finally, toward the end of the war, Rosenberg was appointed deputy minister in charge of repatriation on behalf of the Czechoslovak government.

Rosenberg, as a Jew, managed to accomplish several key missions that ultimately saved hundreds of lives under the personal guidance of President Benes, the World Jewish Congress, the Maccabi World Union, and the British and American governments. This alone provides an interesting perspective as to who Imre Rosenberg really was, and how some of his efforts and actions during the Second World War could easily be deemed heroic. It also explains the meaning behind the four simple words that grace his tombstone at his final resting place in Ottawa, Canada: A Jew in Deed. Through fate and happenstance, Rosenberg managed to attain what most people this day and age strive for: a job that they love doing. Rosenberg wanted to help people. And through performing his job, his duty to his government and the people around him, became just that: "A Jew in Deed."

CHAPTER V

LIBERATION OF THERESIENSTADT

The power of the Holocaust, as a story, is immeasurable. For the six million who perished, for the millions of others, Jewish and non-Jewish, who defied the order of the day and survived, each story, without question, is a powerful entity worthy of its own moment in history. Some stories are well known and have been documented in some form or another by the aggressors, by the observers or by the survivors. Others will never be told, either because they were too difficult to re-enact, or because those that lived them did not survive long enough to share their triumph or horror with others. As many stories about individual and collective experiences of Shoah[6] that exist, thousands if not millions of others will never be formed into images and words for others to share, interpret and understand.

For 301 orphaned Jewish children, their stories exist in their minds, in their hearts, and in documentation that details their remarkable rescue, transfer and rehabilitation at a children's hospice in the English countryside from Theresienstadt concentration camp at the end of the Second World War. For some, the memories consist of vague, fragmented recollections — perhaps the roar of the engines during the flight, the first glimpse of the lush English countryside, the first sight of livestock, or the first time being free. For others, their story is different: the realization that their parents were gone and never coming back, and the sadness of knowing they could never return to their homes or their homeland. But for the 301 orphans rescued from Theresienstadt concentration camp, only one consistent image exists among them. It is that of a small, well-dressed man, either standing in the main courtyard to Terezin conferring with doctors and officials, or standing in the tall grass to the side as the seventeen Royal Air Force planes, transporting the orphans to England rumbled and roared their way down the airstrip.

The flight of the Theresienstadt children and the events that led up to it were distant memories at the end of Rosenberg's life in Canada. Prior to 1985, Rosenberg had never attempted to contact the children whose lives he saved. He also never made any effort to rectify historical records that not only failed to mention his involvement in the rescue and rehabilitation of the 301 Theresienstadt children, but in certain cases failed to recognize that so many children survived the horrors of the camp.

It's difficult to explain why Rosenberg waited so long to tell his side of the story. The most obvious reason he chose to keep quiet for so long was his long-standing effort to let go of his old life in Europe and to focus on his new one as a devoted husband, entrepreneur, academic, philanthropist and painter.

Still, Rosenberg didn't take all the inaccuracies published by various historians and backed by various Jewish and non-Jewish organizations in stride. Indeed, his final project before he died was to tell his story to clarify the historical record and make the inaccuracies known, despite undue criticism from others that his involvement was embellished, if genuine at all.

In 1985, just one year before he died, Rosenberg decided at long last, and with encouragement of his family and friends, to set the record straight and tell his story for the sake of accuracy of Jewish history.

Editor
The Jerusalem Post
The Jerusalem Post Building
Romena, POB 81
Jerusalem, Israel

Re: Research in children surviving Terezin
(Theresienstadt) concentration camp, Czechoslovakia

Dear Sir:
I would like to contact as many of the orphaned children from the above-mentioned camp, as possible. It is now 40 years since the July 1945 flight from Prague Ruzyne airport on 17 Royal Air Force planes. This transport was organized in a great hurry

between the Repatriation Department of the Czechoslovak government and the Home Office in England, because of lack of
proper health facilities in Czechoslovakia at that time.

I was responsible for the flight. Now I am writing the historical
background to a larger study of political rescue activities, during
the Second World War and the immediate postwar period. The
flight forms a part of the record. I am grateful to the editor of your
magazine for publishing this letter.

Sincerely yours,
Dr. I.Y. Rosenberg[7]

No fewer than 60 of the Theresienstadt orphans responded to his
published letter, which also appeared in newspapers in England, the
United States and Canada. Page after page of accounts and memoirs of
the children that survived the horrors of Theresienstadt and who flew
to England to begin new lives made their way to Rosenberg's desk in
Ottawa. Each of the letters told a story that together helped Rosenberg
piece together the events, which led to the flight of the Theresienstadt
orphans that summer morning in 1945, and painted a picture of what
happened to those 301 children after their safe arrival in England.

To accumulate more information, Rosenberg decided to travel to
England to meet with several of the orphans who had formed their
own organization called the '45 Aid Society after the war. Ben
Helfgott, a child survivor of Theresienstadt and director of the '45 Aid
Society, had extended an invitation to Rosenberg to come to London
and meet with some of the other orphan survivors still living there.

"Your letter was passed on to me by Sala Newton,[8] and I simply had
no idea that you played such an important role in the arrangement of
our transport to England," Helfgott wrote to Rosenberg in August,
1985. "I find it even more surprising that 40 years have elapsed, before
we finally caught up with each other. The important thing now is that
we have made contact, and we are really looking forward to meeting
you here in London. You will be made very welcome. I am sure our
members will be delighted to learn from you the background to our
departure from Prague. As you no doubt know, we were in those days

just beginning to wake from a deep slumber. Most of us hardly had much of an education. We were experienced about life, but in other respects we were really terribly ignorant...." [9]

Rosenberg travelled to England and met with several small groups of the now-grown children and their families to exchange information. Helfgott and the others took Rosenberg to museums and on tours, showing him the sights of London. The group spent precious time discussing the common history they shared. In the three weeks Rosenberg spent in London, there was only one brief moment where he was able to discuss the past in any great detail. He returned to Canada extremely hurt and disappointed.

"I think the suspicion if not hostility could have been avoided," Rosenberg wrote in a personal letter to one of the orphans he had met in England, Joshua Herszberg, shortly after his return to Canada. "I was more than once shocked by the doubts expressed as to my motivation, and of course, I felt it was not up to me to respond or to explain. A man at my age does not risk such travel, at his expense, if he were not what he said he was. I certainly did not come to London as a tourist, and I was not interested to see the sights. What I did want were simple facts so that the positive incident of the 301 orphans leaving Terezin for England was saved for Jewish history." [10]

Rosenberg died shortly after his trip to London. He never did amass all the information he was looking for. He also was not able to properly convey his own role in the flight of the orphans and other significant events he was involved in during and after the Second World War, either to the members of the '45 Aid Society or to others. When he finally decided to set the record straight, to explain his involvement that allowed so many lives to continue, his own life ended abruptly.

Let the truth be known that without Rosenberg's involvement, the flight of the Theresienstadt orphans would never have happened. Instead, the 301 child survivors of Hitler's "model" concentration camp would likely have perished from the rampant disease and starvation that afflicted many other inhabitants of the Theresienstadt camp after its liberation. If they somehow had managed to survive, most surely they never would have received the care and attention they did from the devoted Jewish community of England.

Because of the perception of the Holocaust as an inhumane aberration in the course of history, it is clear the state-organized murder of Europe's Jews created its own set of heroes. People were defined as such because their actions were notably different responses to an unusual event in history. What was considered normal behaviour at that time and in that environment had shifted so far to the extreme that in retrospect it is easy to assess an individual's actions as heroic. Since that time, Shoah has documented the most atrocities perpetrated on an individual people in the history of modern humanity.

Historians still debate when the Holocaust actually began and ended. Some argue the war against the Jews began with the passage of anti-Jewish legislation at Nuremberg, in 1935. The so-called Nuremberg laws made it legal for representatives of the German state to round up all persons of Jewish ancestry, remove their possessions, strip them of their rights as citizens of the Reich and separate them from the rest of society. Others argue it began in January 1942, when German military and government leaders met at the Wannsee conference to plan the mass killing of what was calculated to be more than eleven million European Jews. The Wannsee conference in Berlin marked the government's first plan of organized, systematic genocide, using blueprints and other specific criteria to exterminate as many Jews as possible in the most cost and time efficient manner.

Regardless of when it began, the Holocaust changed the scope and perception of Germany and the world. Within that context, those that offered to deter or prevent the mistreatment and murder of Europe's Jews became classified as heroes, according to an unprecedented set of criteria. With that in mind, it is important to recognize that the traditional psychological mechanisms individuals rely on to question the motives, not to mention validity of a person's actions, has to be altered somewhat when examining the Holocaust. Because few methods of keeping accurate, detailed records existed, and because both the actions and reactions of people were so completely warped by war, individuals' tales of the Holocaust have to be greeted with a certain sense of acceptance.

As a high-ranking official of the Czechoslovak government-in-exile, Rosenberg had every opportunity during the Second World War and the Nazi occupation of Europe to avoid persecution, escape death and shape his own destiny in whichever way he chose. Unlike more than six million other Jews during the Second World War, Rosenberg, through planned circumstances and luck, found himself in a position few Jews could only dream of, which was being safe and having choices.

Yet, despite the fortunate and highly unusual position he found himself in, he still chose to defy the odds and do everything within his power to influence that government and their British hosts to save Jewish lives. By convincing the Czechoslovak government to condone his dual role as both a deputy minister and a committed member of several pro-Jewish and pro-Zionist causes, Rosenberg fulfilled his personal commitment to help others in need.

When that period in his life came to an abrupt conclusion in 1949, he found little reason to or fulfillment in telling his story and making others aware of his own efforts. Because the Second World War was a period of such intense chaos, it was often the case that specific records of events, transactions and communications weren't written down. In some cases, this is difficult to believe, since Hitler's plan to exterminate the Jewish people and identity and make Germany the dominant power of Europe is so well documented. Hitler and his supporters ordered thousands of films, documents and other forms of evidence, destroyed toward the end of the war. Mountains of primary material and secondary accounts from the Nazi regime and other people and places, sit in Jewish museums and historical archives today, as evidence that the Holocaust did happen.

Nonetheless, not all aspects of the Second World War were as well documented as the Nazi plan. Favours, handshakes, bribes and verbal agreements were often the preferred method for obtaining fake passports and travel documents and for getting work permits extended, train tickets, food, clothing, money, shelter and anything that could be obtained. Second-World-War Europe was not a place or time where individuals filled out forms and followed the book to get what they wanted.[110]

While that type of behaviour is typically associated with individuals' actions to help themselves, it can also be applied, particularly in the context of the Second World War and the Holocaust, to plans and actions put forth by individuals to help save others. It's not uncommon to hear testimony from people or groups of both Jewish and non-Jewish affiliation about individuals who hid entire Jewish families to protect them from being sent to concentration camps, or who provided money, fake documents and passports to those who couldn't obtain legitimate help through the usual channels. There are also records with the Zionist Archives, the Jewish Agency in Palestine and hundreds of other Jewish and non-Jewish organizations that helped Jews during the Second World War. They contain large sections of primary materials that do not back up the claims of many people who were involved in helping others during that time. Yet those claims are real, and have been substantiated through the testimony of those who benefited from the kindness and generosity of others.

Rosenberg was one of those individuals. While he used his position of authority to help others in need, often legitimately, many positive things he did during that time weren't documented. His role in arranging seventeen Royal Air Force training planes to transport the Theresienstadt orphans from Prague to England was more a series of personal negotiations than an official part of his role as repatriation minister for the Czechoslovak government.

No records, either at various Jewish and government archives or at the RAF historical branch in London, show that the actual flight took place on the day and time it supposedly did. Nonetheless, hundreds of pages of testimony confirm that the Theresienstadt orphans made their way to England by plane. The sources include the Theresienstadt orphans themselves and bits of pieces of documents from the archives of the World Jewish Congress. The United Nations Relief and Rehabilitation Association, the National Agency in Palestine, the American Jewish Joint Distribution Committee or "Joint," the Red Cross, the British Home Office, the British Embassy in Prague and many other archival sources were involved. Many of those documents, while not part of the existing historical account, also confirm who helped them get there: Imre Yitzhak Rosenberg.

CHAPTER VI

THE MODEL CAMP

Depending on how history is recorded, an event can often overshadow the individual who organized it. Sometimes, the event is so horrific and overwhelming, that it only makes sense to blame it on one individual or a small group of people. Other times, the event itself is so overwhelmingly positive that the individual who somehow made it all happen is lost in the moment.

So it happened that Imre Rosenberg was not credited with helping save the remaining children of Theresienstadt at the end of the Second World War and giving them a second chance to live. Rosenberg enlisted the help of the Royal Air Force, the U.S. army, the British Central Office for Refugees and other British, American and Jewish relief organizations to arrange for the safe passage of the orphaned children to England from Theresienstadt in the summer of 1945. He has never, to this day, been recognized for his efforts.

At the same time, the children who eventually grew up and moved on to Israel, Canada, the U.S., Australia and elsewhere never really thought to question how the seventeen RAF planes found their way to the tarmac at Ruzyne airport outside Prague. It didn't really matter to them. They were leaving war-torn Europe. They were leaving their memories of death, destruction and chaos behind for new lives with new families. It didn't matter to them how they got there, only that they were going to a better place.

If a scale had existed to measure the viciousness and brutality of the various detainment and concentration camps the Nazi government created between 1938 and 1945, Theresienstadt would have been at the lower end of the list. Being the model camp used by the Nazis to show the world how Jews were being detained during the war made it one of the least horrific detainment centres in Europe at t he time. Nevertheless, conditions of death and destruction existed at

Theresienstadt, as they did at every other concentration camp, in a different, less obvious form.

Theresienstadt was a ghetto, a concentration camp and a way station for Western European Jews en route to Auschwitz, between 1941 and 1945. Located about forty miles north of Prague, the small Czech village became the site of SS leader Reinhard Heydrich's model concentration camp. In contrast to other concentration camps set up by the Germans during the war, Theresienstadt was not known as a death camp. Instead, it was set up as a temporary holding area for Jews who were moved from parts of Western Europe to the Eastern death camps. To make room for the 90,000 Jews that were detained in Theresienstadt during its four-year existence, Heydrich expelled the 7,000 non-Jews who had called the tiny town home. Once the region was isolated with barbed wire fences, guards and trenches, the Germans began deporting some 144,000 Czech, Dutch, German and Danish Jews to its confines.

Because so many secularized Western Jews from the cosmopolitan cities of Europe were deported there, Theresienstadt gave rise to a rich social and literary culture. Some of the most prominent Czech, Austrian and German artists, writers, scientists, musicians and professors, at one point or another, were incarcerated there. For Jews facing deportation, word spread quickly that Theresienstadt was more of a detainment centre than a labour or death camp. Some German and Danish Jews bribed officials to be sent there. Some even arrived at the gates dressed in elegant suits or dresses, innocently asking for appropriate accommodation.

With 90,000 Jews living in a space vacated by the 7,000 former inhabitants, they were quickly and decisively stripped of their illusions. Disease was rampant, food scarce and living conditions, underneath the surface, substandard. By 1942, almost 16,000 Jews died from disease, starvation or extreme cruelty. To dispose of the bodies, the Germans constructed a crematorium within the camp capable of handling 190 bodies a day and 69,000 a year.

Still, because so many secularized, educated Jews passed through its gates, a rich cultural life emerged that was unique from any other concentration camp. A lending library circulated more than 60,000 books. Symphonies and plays were performed on a regular basis. Children attended classes, participated in sports and cultural activities and were encouraged to explore art and science. During the day, Jewish artists painted what was acceptable to their Nazi overseers in specially constructed ghetto workshops. At night, however, many of them secretly painted a true reflection of what life in Theresienstadt was like, hiding their works in ghetto walls, paint cans and other undetectable places.

In 1943, Theresienstadt became the focus of international attention when the Danish government, one of very few concerned with the fate of their Jewish citizens who were deported by the Nazis, demanded an accounting of the fate of their citizens through the International Red Cross. The Red Cross requested to visit the camp to confirm the Jews were being detained and treated in accordance with the Geneva Convention. The German government permitted the visit, though not before more than two-thirds of the Jews living in the camp were deported to Auschwitz and the grounds were cleaned, painted and beautified to resemble the "model" camp. Heydrich even went so far as to arrange for a monument to be erected to honour dead Jews. Needless to say, the "model camp" created by the Germans succeeded in convincing the world, for a time, at least, that rumours of mass killings, tortures, scientific experiments and other atrocities were unfounded.

Rosenberg entered Theresienstadt in 1945 to open the gates and deal with the ravages of Nazi cruelty.

CHAPTER VII

THE ROAD TO THERESIENSTADT

Of all the concentration camps known from the Second World War, Theresienstadt is not one of the more notable camps. Most who have studied the German campaign to annihilate the Jewish people know of such camps as Auschwitz, Bergen-Belsen, Birkenau, Dauchau and others, which figure prominently in many survivors' testimonies of the Holocaust and in most historical accounts of that era. Part of the reason Theresienstadt was and still is less known among its sisters is because it was not a death camp. For most of its five-year life span the grounds of Theresienstadt were used primarily as a holding tank for Jews and other non-Aryans before being transported to the more notable camps for forced labour, death or both.

There are some ideas in life that seem so small and simple to organize and arrange, that can develop into an enormously complex and taxing struggle to accomplish. Dealing with Europe's eighteen million refugees at the end of the Second World War was complicated enough. The hundreds of thousands of individual arrangements organized and planned through countless volunteers, agencies, and government sources are too numerous to mention. By 1944, Rosenberg had progressed enough in the ranks of the Czech government-in-exile to be appointed an official in charge of the soon-to-be-liberated territories of Czechoslovakia. His prime mandate, according to President Benes, was to handle all aspects of the Jewish rehabilitation in the liberated territories of Czechoslovakia. His first trip in this capacity was to Moscow, where Rosenberg led a delegation of both Jewish and non-Jewish representatives to negotiate with the Russian Red Army on the fate of Czechoslovakia after the war. Rosenberg's role was to secure the safety of the Jews once the Russians liberated his homeland. While that never materialized, Rosenberg was able to negotiate successfully with the executive of the Soviet Jewish Anti-Fascist Committee to have them join other nations within the

World Jewish Congress. The Soviet government, while against Stalin's principles of non-religion, endorsed the Soviet committee, for the simple reason that Stalin thought he would be able to mobilize world Jewish support in his fight against Hitler, if he condoned one of their larger organizations in Russia. That never quite materialized either, even though Soviet recognition of Israel as a Jewish homeland took place.

From Moscow, Rosenberg arranged for a rescue and rehabilitation convoy with the help of Soviet authorities, which wound its way through Eastern Europe, Germany, Poland and beyond. He travelled in Soviet military pickup trucks to every concentration camp liberated by the Red Army, establishing refugee checkpoints at each camp and also in nearby towns to help Jews register as refugees, obtain travel documents, seek medical attention, and share information about missing friends and relatives. One of his main tasks was to organize a reporting system in Moscow, Lwow and Hust to provide names of surviving Jews to organizations in London, New York and Jerusalem, who would then update their lists and attempt to inform family members of their relatives' whereabouts. That task prompted Rosenberg to broadcast details of events and conditions in postwar Europe and "A" lists of survivors via radio, which he transmitted daily through the Jewish Telegraphic Agency around the world.[12]

As the Soviet army pushed the front westward and as Germany retreated closer to the Americans and British approaching from the East, Rosenberg tagged along with the Russian Red Army. He spent his days and nights bumping along bombed-out roads across the decimated Eastern European countryside, establishing offices of the Czech Repatriation Department in every new border point with Poland, Hungary, Austria and Germany.

Rosenberg later recalled: "I couldn't figure out for the life of me how I ended up in the back of a Soviet military convoy, speeding through the frigid Polish countryside, expecting a group of German patriots to jump out of the trees at any moment and attack. I slept little and talked even less. The soldiers didn't understand why I was there and viewed me as a burden to their mission. I overheard one of them discussing with another as to how it would be easier to leave me behind in the Polish countryside, except they would surely be dismissed from their posts if

Moscow found out about it, or so they said. They didn't know I could understand Russian."[13]

Between January and May 1945, Rosenberg established no less than 112 repatriation offices across Eastern and Central Europe. He received and distributed more than fifty million Czechoslovak crowns to Jewish camp survivors and arranged for food, clothing, identity documents and railway tickets for the more than 1,000 refugees that passed through his checkpoints each day. According to various telegrams between Rosenberg, the Allied High Command, UNRRA, the International Refugee Board and the Joint, he arranged for trains and other modes of transport for Europe's Jews to travel back to their home towns and villages.

It was mid-spring 1945, by the time Rosenberg returned to Prague from his mission across Europe. On May 9, Rosenberg set up a repatriation office in Prague to handle the massive amounts of paperwork and other administrative duties relating to the other refugee sites he had established in other parts of the country and beyond. This office was one of the first offices to be re-established under Benes's direction in postwar Czechoslovakia. With the help of the government, Rosenberg was able to secure a small staff and an even smaller budget to help the flood of Jewish refugees now desperately trying either to resettle somewhere in Europe or make arrangements to leave for Palestine or North America. Two days later, he went to Theresienstadt to take over its administration from the Soviet army.

"We felt that liberation was very near," 18-year-old Lipa Tepper, one of the child survivors of Theresienstadt, later recalled. "One day I was standing near the wire fence with some people when a group of Czech partisans passed by, and one of them called out to us that the Russians would be there the following morning. I thought it was all a load of rubbish. I did not believe it, and I gave it no more thought. I went back to my barracks and went to sleep.

"The following morning, early on May 9, somebody said to me there was a Russian tank in the camp and I said, "Look, forget about it, you are dreaming." "No," he said, "There really is a Russian tank in the camp." I went out and there it was, a Russian tank with Russian soldiers standing on top of it.

"The whole camp started buzzing and people came out, and the Russians were throwing biscuits. After that a group of people went out to town, and they came back with a horse and cart with food and provisions on it. They brought sardines, salami and bread. People were climbing all over the cart trying to get some food. I managed to get some salami, and I went back to my bunk and sat down and ate it. There seemed to have been a lot of people who ate too many things too quickly, and then a dysentery epidemic broke out in the camp, and the Russians quarantined us. We were not allowed out, which was a very bad thing, because we could not go out to the town to get some food. But people seemed to go under the wire and go out and get food. We survived anyway."[14]

"The conditions were deplorable," Rosenberg scribbled on the back page torn from a book. "Corpses littered the ground along the fences and the barracks. Those that were still alive were nothing but skin and bones. It was clear these people were not well. We were informed before our arrival that a cholera epidemic had already engulfed many of the camp's 30,000 known survivors. I wired the Repatriation Office in London for backup personnel to assist in documenting the survivors and providing them with food, medicine and proper clothing to ensure they would be fit to leave the camps as soon as possible."[15]

When Rosenberg arrived at Theresienstadt that warm spring morning, he knew to expect the worst. After his travels through Russia, Poland and the Balkans, he had grown accustomed to seeing misery, despair and defeat. When he walked through the gates of Theresienstadt with his small entourage of volunteers and helpers, Rosenberg knew it wasn't going to be a pretty sight.

"I'd never seen anything like it," Rosenberg recalled. "Amid all the sickness and degradation, a small line of men and women, no more than ten or twelve of them, were standing alongside the fence near the front gate of the camp with what at first glance looked like garbage, orderly lined up in from of them. Several of the men were dressed in suits, overcoats and hats, their prison garb conspicuously peeking beneath their trouser legs and jacket arms. The women wore dresses and hats, many of them in tattered pieces that dwarfed their emaciated bodies. All of them were filthy to the core, standing in line with their bags and other belongings in front of them, as if waiting for the next train to Munich. Just then, a series of shouts in Dutch caught my attention. Two women were arguing over a piece of tattered baggage, wrenching it back and forth between them like a Mexican piñata, yelling at the top of their lungs about who the sack belonged to. As I approached them, one of the women looked at me, and at the same moment, lost her balance, as the other woman ripped the bag from her hands. She fell to the ground. I rushed to help her to her feet, but she refused to move. She was in complete shock. The other woman just stood there, defiantly clutching the bag, refusing to bend down and help the other woman. Looking back on that moment, I realized that particular scene in no other way possible explained the circumstances of Terezin."[16]

"I remember hanging out with a couple of the other boys behind some of the wooden outhouses about fifty feet to the right of the front gates," recalled Samuel Hilton, one of the child survivors of the camp. He was fifteen at the time. "We watched this little short guy walk in through the gates with a clipboard underneath his arm. He was wearing a uniform that wasn't German and wasn't Russian and he looked uncomfortably hot. We weren't sure exactly what the uniform was, since me and the two other guys I was with were Polish. We'd never seen a Czech uniform before.

"This man walks into the camp with a group of maybe ten or fifteen people. They were talking idly to the Russians, looking around and smoking cigarettes. The little guy walks up to the two of the Russians starts talking to them, looking around every once in a while at all the people, who, of course, are staring right back at him. He looked uncomfortable, from what I remember. So he finishes talking with the two Russian guys and went back to his buddies, and they brought out these little tables and start putting papers and pens out on them. We think it's another round of deportations and we can't move, I mean, we didn't know what to think. We managed to sneak out of the camp a couple of times in the week or so since the Russians took over, since as far as we knew the war was over. I remember us talking about how we could sneak back out of the camp and run away. It turns out this Czech guy was trying to set up a roll call so he could find out how many people were in the camp and what their names were, so we went and signed up. The only other time I saw that guy was when we got off the bus at the airport to get on to the planes to go to England. He was there, in the same uniform. I remember him because his ears stuck out from under his hat, like they were the only things keeping his hat on his head. I never saw him again after I got on the plane."[17]

Litzi Sonnenschein, also an orphan survivor of Theresienstadt, recalled a similar experience the day the camp was liberated.

"I was very young, five years old at the time, and some of the other prisoners used to take a small group of us to the yard to play. We would build little towns with roads and shops out of rocks and sticks and other things, and pretend there were people shopping and eating on terraces and things like that. I remember that day in particular because the adults that used to watch us play suddenly disappeared. I was playing with two or three of the other girls, and one of them looked up and there was no one there. We all started to cry, I guess because we thought the Germans had taken them away. So many people disappeared from the camp, especially towards the end, that it seemed like every day someone would vanish. I remember running with two other girls across the courtyard to the infirmary because one of us thought maybe Mrs. Stein, one of the women who used to watch us, got sick and was in the infirmary. Halfway across the courtyard a woman stopped us. She was crying and talking really fast, and I don't recall who she was, but I remember what she told us. She told us we were free. We would be allowed to leave, and we could go to Israel and do whatever we wanted.

"I don't remember much in between the time we were supposedly liberated and the time we flew to England. It seemed that everything was the same, except there was more food, and we were allowed to roam around a lot more than before. I also remember going for tests, being inspected for lice and getting a shot, which I remember quite vividly because it really hurt!"[18]

The first few days at Theresienstadt were trying for Rosenberg. There was no food, no medicine, no doctors, and the constant threat of disease. At his request, the army had barricaded the front gate, sealing the camp to prevent infected survivors from wandering outside the camp and spreading illness to the nearby towns. However, many of the prisoners had managed to slip through the wired fence anyway, and the Russians did little to stop them. A week earlier, an international Red Cross committee had arrived at the camp with several Czechoslovak health workers. Together they tried to contain the sudden wave of dysentery and spotted fever that had emerged among the inmates. But with no supplies and no back up on the way, their efforts had a minimal effect.

"I had some of the volunteers set up small tables to begin the process of documenting each person's family name." Rosenberg later explained in a letter to Sophie Caplan, a personal friend and one of the Theresienstadt orphans he later contacted in an effort to write his story of the flight of the orphans. "The purpose of the exercise was to officially declare them refugees, obtain assistance for them, and also to provide for them travel papers to allow them to return to their homes. From the look on some of their faces, it seemed they thought we had ulterior motives in mind. It was easy to see why they might think we were part of the German army setting up another deportation roll call!"[19]

One of the first things Rosenberg noticed about the camp was how ill the inmates were. He quickly learned that the last shipment of Jews, who arrived from the East as the German troops had retreated a week earlier, had brought with them dysentery and typhus, which had quickly spread among the weak and malnourished population of the camp.

"Due to the physical conditions of health, lack of food supplies, and non-availability of medical doctors and medicines in the first weeks after Theresienstadt liberation, I was forced to make immediately drastic and radical decisions to protect and save the lives of the survivors." Rosenberg wrote the following to Sala Newton, one of the survivors of Terezin, in August 1985.

"I kept noticing the children. They seemed to have no supervision other than each other, and despite the obvious differences in ages, they all generally stuck together as one cohesive group. It didn't take me long to realize that the health and safety of those children, who I quickly learned were virtually all orphans, was in serious danger. I had to come up with some kind of arrangement to have the children moved from the camp before it was too late for them all."[20]

CHAPTER VIII

THE FLIGHT OF THE ORPHANS

"A transport of 301 children from the former concentration camp of Theresienstadt in Czechoslovakia arrived last week at a British airport. The children are between the ages of 3 and 16, and all of them have lived in concentration camps for many months or even years. They have lost contact with their parents and most of them are probably orphans."[21]

From the Zionist Review, London, August 24, 1945.

Rosenberg had not planned on putting children who had just emerged from the hell of the Second World War onto British transport planes and shipping them to England for rehabilitation. After all, in an era where supplies and resources were scarce, flying children out of concentration camps paled in importance to flying in relief supplies and personnel to help thousands of Jewish refugees. Rosenberg's initial idea was to arrange for a motor convoy to pick up the children and transport them either to Ruzyne, the closest town to Theresienstadt, or to Prague, where they would receive better medical and personal attention than at the camp. What mattered to Rosenberg was not where but how quickly the children could be moved away from the concentration camp to an environment that would allow them to recover both mentally and physically. On May 18, 1945, Rosenberg began the complicated task of arranging for the Terezin children to be moved from the camp to a more suitable environment.

Rosenberg sent a telegram that read as follows:

Re: orphan children of Theresienstadt. It is essential that medical personnel be sent to treat the children and prepare them for departure as soon as possible. Ask Foreign Office to telegraph our Ambassador in Prague to report on the above and send a copy

direct to Dr. Sturdee at the Ministry of Health. Also request that
Dr. Klinger, resident doctor of President Benes, come to
Theresienstadt to inspect and certify the children's health before
their departure. Travel arrangements must be secured, as well as
temporary shelter. Inquires appreciated. I. J. Rosenberg.[22]

With one single telegram, Rosenberg launched a complicated
sequence of events that would eventually lead to the flight of 301
orphan Jewish children from Terezin to England. His first task was to
isolate the children and arrange for medical treatment to cure them of
dysentery, typhus, lice and other contagious diseases, which were
infecting the inmates of the camp. Rosenberg sent a telegram to the
Czechoslovak repatriation office, still in London, requesting that
arrangements be made to send medical supplies and a doctor to the
camp to inspect the children. The Czech government, in collaboration
with a Mr. Prestige, then secretary of the Home Office in London,
became aware of Rosenberg's intentions and immediately contacted
Dr. Klinger, President Benes's resident physician, to advise him of
Rosenberg's request.

Dr. Klinger agreed to travel to Theresienstadt to inspect the children
and prepare official documents to allow them to leave the camp for
another country. Neither Dr. Klinger nor Rosenberg knew for certain
where the children would eventually be taken. They did know, however, that no government or agency would accept them without a clean
bill of health.

A few discreet inquires launched by the Jewish Relief Agency in
London had quickly revealed that Jewish communities in Prague and
Amsterdam were unable to set up proper facilities to care for the children. Without Rosenberg's knowledge, the Home Office in London
contacted Mrs. Madeline Nathan of UNRRA to request her help in
locating and making appropriate arrangements for the transfer of the
children to a more safe and secure environment. Mrs. Nathan sent a
telegram to Miss Ruth Fellner at Windermere Estate, a large country
estate in Calgarth outside London, to help rehabilitate children after
the war. They asked that arrangements be made to care for the chil-

dren if the appropriate papers and arrangements could be made to transport them from Theresienstadt to England. Fellner accepted, securing the location to which the children would be moved, once they were in suitable health to travel and that approval could be arranged for their entry into England. The only problem that remained was how to get the children across the English Channel to the Windermere Estate.

Another telegram was sent that read as follows:

From Prague to Foreign Office: Please pass the following to Fellner Central Refugees Committee from Mrs. Nathan. Re orphaned children, we have secured lodging but no transport. Air attaché has been consulted with a possible small group of children to be air lifted at intervals. Approval may not be obtained.[23]

Rosenberg later admitted that it hadn't occurred to him that he had to organize the airplanes to transfer the orphans to England. He had assumed the children would have to be moved somewhere else in Central Europe, either by motorcade, train or even boat, if necessary. When he heard that Nathan, through her various contacts at UNRRA and other organizations, had tried unsuccessfully to arrange for British bomber planes to fly the children from Prague to Carlisle, he thought of another way.

On May 3, 1945, in a letter to Czechoslovak Repatriation Minister Jan Becko, Rosenberg asked that the government request the use of training planes, rather than bombers, from the British government to help transport the orphans from Prague to the Windermere Estate in Calgarth. The closest airport to the Esstate was in Carlisle, about thirty kilometres south. It was agreed that this would be the most suitable place for the drop-off to occur.

Rather than force the British government to incur the cost of flying its own planes over the British Channel across to Czechoslovakia and back, Rosenberg suggested the Czech government urge the British Home Office to use different planes. The planes would bring a large section of the Czechoslovak air force, stationed in England, back to

Prague and then take the children on the return journey. Rosenberg
sent a similar letter to the London branch of the Jewish Relief Agency,
hoping to muster support, and place pressure on the English government to allow the use of RAF planes for a non-military task.

The next telegram read as follows:

> Requesting on behalf of Czech Repatriation Department the use
> of RAF training planes to return Czech air pilots to Prague. Stop.
> Also request planes be used to transport children back to Carlisle,
> England. Stop. Arrangements for pickup to be handled there.
> End.[24]

At the same time, Rosenberg sent a telegram to the Home Office
in London, requesting that visas be issued for "about 300 German,
Austrian or Polish orphans under sixteen from Theresienstadt camp" in
order to grant them legitimate passage to England.[25] Still, because of
the unusual nature of the transfer, and because details concerning how
the children would arrive in England and in what condition were
sketchy, Rosenberg's request was initially turned down by the Home
Office, for those reasons and because there were far more orphan survivors in the camp than originally thought.

Initial reports suggested that 50 orphans had been found in
Theresienstadt, which the Czechoslovak government and the Home
Office were willing to make arrangements to transfer. However, when
the Home Office heard there were as many as 300 orphan survivors in
the camp, arrangements became more complicated.

> Dear Warner,
> You will remember that I told you last week that the Central
> Office for Refugees were sending a representative to Prague to
> discuss with the Czech government the transfer of some
> 50 orphans found in Theresienstadt camp. You were going to
> inform our Minister that we were prepared to admit them to this
> country.
>   The representative has now returned and reported, and the
> arrangements are well underway. We had expressed concern that

the number of orphans far exceeded what was previously determined, which delayed action. In fact, there turns out to be nearly 300 orphans under the age of 16, and we would appreciate it if you would now telegraph to our Minister at Prague as follows:

1. Home Office has agreed to the admission of about 300 German, Austrian or Polish orphans under 16 from Theresienstadt camp, provided that they are passed as medically fit by a doctor approved by the British Embassy.
2. Doctor I.J. Rosenberg, Deputy Director for Repatriation, Czech government, is understood to be arranging for transportation, which should if possible be to a London airport.
3. Essential that at least 48 hours clear notice (excluding Sundays) be given to Home Office and to Central Office for Refugees before arrival of each party, in order that proper measures of reception and disposal may be arranged.

C.F.A. Warner, Esq., C.M.G.,
Foreign Office[26]

After several persistent telegrams to his government's office in Prague, who in turn sent strong urgings to the British government authorities in London, Rosenberg obtained approval to transfer the children without visas to England, as long as their medical condition was stable and verified by Dr. Klinger.

On July 6, 1945, almost two months after Rosenberg's arrival, he received a copy of a telegram from the Foreign Office to Prague, which stated the following:

Home Office has agreed to the admission of about 300 orphans under 16 years of age from the Theres0nstadt camp, provided that they are passed as medically fit by a doctor approved by the British Embassy. Doctor I.J. Rosenberg, Deputy Director in Repatriation, Czech Government, will be arranging with the British Embassy in Prague for transportation....[27]

As the days and weeks passed and the condition of the children and other inmates of Theresienstadt slowly improved, preparations began to emerge as to how and when the transfer of the orphans would take place. Dr. Klinger had arrived with a small staff to assist the Red Cross and other personnel in the camp in treating the survivors. The quarantine of the camp remained in effect, though the outbreak of typhus and dysentery had dramatically subsided.[28]

Rosenberg worked in the camp each day, establishing lists of names and arranging for those lists to be sent to the Joint and other organizations to help survivors find their immediate families. At night, he stayed in nearby Prague so he could be in close contact with regional authorities to ensure that negotiations between the British Home Office, the British Embassy in Prague, the Joint, UNRRA and others continued expeditiously, concerning how the flight of the orphans would take place and when.

Meanwhile, Rosenberg learned that the British government had decided to allow a total of 1,000 orphan children from various concentration camps throughout Europe to enter England. Of those, 300 would come from Theresienstadt and the rest from Poland and the Ukraine. The Home Office and UNRRA were making separate arrangements for the arrival and care of the other children.

Rosenberg confided the following in a letter to his long-time friend, Erica Barber, in 1970. "I could have been wrong, but I think the Terezin flight may have had something to do with similar arrangements being made for additional orphaned children from other camps to be flown to England. But I'm not smug enough or arrogant enough to assume so unless proven otherwise."[29]

By late July, with the exception of a few minor complications, the arrangements had been set. Three hundred children from Theresienstadt, along with fifteen relief workers in the camp supplied by the British Home Office, were to leave the camp on Tuesday, July 31, 1945. The planes, which held members of the Czechoslovak air force, were scheduled to land at Ruzyne Airport outside Prague, unload the officers, refuel, load up the children and return to an airstrip at Carlisle in southern England. One brief complication arose when the fifteen escorts chosen by Rosenberg and the Red Cross to accompany the children on the flight were suddenly moved to Hungary and could not be used as chaperones for the trip. The Home Office immediately arranged for new escorts. The children were to leave Theresienstadt, on August 2, and travel by train to Prague, where they would stay at the Belgitska Street Hostel and await the arrival of the British training planes.

While the children anxiously awaited their trip in Prague, an equally anxious group of women frantically made last-minute arrangements for the children's arrival at the Windermere Estate at Calgarth. The Jewish Refugee Committee in London had arranged for the transfer of 1,000 orphaned Jewish children, and the first 300 from Theresienstadt were to arrive at Windermere in a matter of days. During the Second World War, Windermere had been converted into a small makeshift village for the employees of a nearby aircraft factory. The bungalows on the estate were still occupied by employees' families, but there were a number of blocks containing small semi-enclosed rooms with bunk beds. There was also a central building consisting of a large restaurant, an entertainment hall and offices. Situated on the shore of Lake Windermere and surrounded by woods and fields, the estate seemed an appropriate place to rehabilitate the children.[30]

On August 8, Rosenberg received a telegram in Prague from the British Embassy that everything was on schedule, with the aircraft expected to leave Prague the next morning at 11 a.m. and arrive at the airport in Carlisle at 5 p.m. The estimated time of arrival at Windermere was 8 p.m. He went back to his hotel in Prague to wait for the planes to arrive.

It wouldn't be that simple. Just after midnight on August 9, Rosenberg received another telegram, this time from his government's office in London, advising that the flight had been delayed twenty-four hours because of inclement weather over the English Channel. Rosenberg received a brief telegram at his hotel advising him of the delay.

The telegram read as follows:

If weather improves the departure will be on August 10th. Suggest you keep in touch with the airfield in Prague. Ends.[31]

That same weather system held back the planes for another four days. The children were restless, tired and still malnourished, even though they had had several months to rest and recover. Finally, on August 13, 1945, the weather broke, and the children assembled outside the hostel in Prague to make the final leg of their journey to the Ruzyne airport and eventually to England. The children were taken by bus to the Ruzyne airfield, just west of the city. The planes were waiting on the airstrip, ready to fly the children to a new home and life.

"I certainly remember the plane ride, because it was very noisy and bumpy, and I was sick on the plane," recalled Litzi Sonnenschein. She had just turned six at the time of the flight. "From the window of the plane, I could see all the little squares that I guess were farms in the French countryside, and then the water of the English Channel and then England. Now it seems like it all happened in a matter of days, but I guess it really was more like months."[32]

"The plane ride? How could I forget!" exclaimed Samuel Hilton, another of the Theresienstadt orphan survivors. "I remember the trip to Prague, I remember waiting for three days for the planes to arrive. I remember feeling really scared that the whole thing was just a joke and we'd have to go back to Terezin, or worse, be sent to Auschwitz. It was weird, because those extra days made me really wonder where I wanted to go and what I was going to do with my life. As it turned out, it gave me some time to decide if I really wanted to go to Israel. I ended up deciding during those three days to join my aunt and uncle, who were living in California. It took a while, but eventually, after some time in London, I got my papers to go to California and live there. I spent the rest of my life there, and I've had a great life.

"As for the plane ride, I remember that a lot of the other kids were really sick. It was a terrible flight, very bumpy. There weren't any seats or anything on the planes. They were big empty training planes designed to hold cargo or something, I guess. One of the chaperones that came with us on the trip let me sit for a while in the bottom of the plane where the plastic turret was, and I could see underneath the clouds what seemed to be all of Europe. It was my first time in a plane, and I loved it. Maybe that's why I ended up joining the U.S. air force later on. I know that's probably one of the most vivid memories I have of the entire war and the Holocaust."[33]

"Finally my anxiety to remove as many as possible of the healthy children away from danger was coming true," Rosenberg recalled in a letter to one of the orphans, Sophie Caplan, recounting his interpretation of the flight. "The most fascinating part of the entire episode happened as the children were boarding the plane. A lady came to me at the last moment, as I was helping the children through the cargo doors, and presented me with a three- or four-year-old boy who was an orphan from another camp and asked me whether that boy could go along to England as well. To each ten children there was an escort of two adults. And so I took him, put him on the plane, and that brought the total number of children to 301. It was a great day and a sight to remember when one fine August morning seventeen Royal Air Force training planes took off with 301 Terezin orphans between the ages of three and sixteen to a new life. It was one of the highlights of my postwar activities."[34]

This act of kindness caused a serious problem when the planes arrived in Carlisle five hours later.

"A slight complication arose as the planes began to come in," wrote Brown and Don in *Evacuation to Westmoreland*, in 1946. "Instead of the load of 300 children and two adults, it was found that there were 301 children on board the first plane. [sic] As the plane was leaving the Ruzyne airfield, a Czech official placed a boy, whose chaperone had heard of this trip to England, on the plane. The boy had stowed away on the plane. He had, of course, not undergone any quarantine or observation and 0was venomous. The boy was detained in the Carlisle

isolation hospital, and the 300 children who had travelled with him
were isolated."[35]

The boy, after being treated for dysentery and malnutrition, was
eventually sent to join the other children at Windermere.

> "I have just returned from a visit to the Calgarth Hostel,
> Windermere, where 300 Jewish boys and girls, survivors of Nazi
> death camps, arrived some days ago," wrote a British Jewish
> Chronicle correspondent, in August 1945. "They are the first batch
> being brought over here by permission of the Government. They
> were imprisoned in Theresienstadt concentration camp. They are
> here in England to recuperate, and are being taken care of by the
> Central British Fund for Jewish Relief and Rehabilitation. Fifty of
> the 300 are girls. Seventeen are aged three to seven; twenty are 8
> to 12; fifty are 13 to 14 and the rest are 15 and over. One child,
> aged 3, was a stowaway, bringing the total number of children to
> 301. I was surprised that these children looked so healthy after all
> they had been through."[36]

CHAPTER IX

So ended Rosenberg's Jewish activities in Second-World-War Europe. He remained in Prague as an official with the Czech government up to the Communist coup in March 1948, continuing with his duties of helping Jewish refugees obtain financial assistance and identification papers to migrate to where they wanted to go without having to escape. At the same time, Rosenberg refocused his efforts with the Joint, the Maccabi World Union and the Jewish Agency in Palestine in lobbying the British government to open emigration to Israel and establish the British-controlled region as a Jewish state.

In 1946, still as an official of the Czech government, Rosenberg participated in one of the first United Jewish Appeal drives in the United States. He arrived in New York to a fanfare of media who were aware of his efforts in Europe to help save lives and repatriate Jews. He spoke on the same platform as Eleanor Roosevelt and other notable figures on the importance of committing funds to distribute to needy Jews worldwide.

In May 1948, he was tried in absentia and sentenced to life imprisonment by the newly established Communist courts in Prague for Zionist and pro-American activities.

"Canada wasn't Imre's first choice of places to emigrate to," Truda Rosenberg recalled about her husband's story of how he came to live in Ottawa. "After he found out he had been tried and convicted in absentia by the Communist Czech government, he fled to Brussels. The Communist authorities followed him there, but Imre escaped to the Canadian Embassy, where they arranged for him to get a temporary visa to stay in London. I think he went to the Canadian Embassy because it was close to the hotel he was staying at in Brussels, and also because he had worked with several Canadians before and knew they could be trusted. Also, he was good friends with Mr. Nemec, at that time the Czech Ambassador in Canada, who was willing to sponsor him to come to Canada as a political refugee. I don't think he ever expected to permanently move to Canada. He needed protection from the Communist authorities who were after him."[37]

Rosenberg had indeed wanted to immigrate to Israel, the region he had spent much of his life fighting for and supporting on so many different levels. However, by the time he had finished his postwar duties and arranged for thousands of refugees to receive proper documentation to allow them to enter the British-controlled region of Palestine, there weren't any certificates left. Because the British mandate limited the number of Jews allowed into Palestine, Rosenberg was forced to look into other options.

He managed to get to London. But he couldn't stay long because the now-Communist government was pressuring British authorities to find Rosenberg and allow them to extradite him back to the Czech Republic.

"So one of Nemec's last duties as ambassador to the old Czech government was to sponsor my husband to come to Canada," explained Truda. "I don't think he ever wanted or expected to come here, and even if he did, I'm certain he never expected to stay as long as he did. I think he also felt that if he couldn't go to Israel and he couldn't stay in Europe, he would have a much easier time and be more connected here in North America. That's not to say he didn't love Canada, as he participated extensively in Jewish, academic and other activities in an extensive way and eventually became a Canadian citizen. He made a home and a life for himself here, even though it happened by circumstance."[38]

On March 3, 1949, after travelling across the Atlantic on the *Ascania*, he arrived in Halifax, Nova Scotia, with a single bag and a few dollars in his pocket. Since his friend Frantisek Nemec was in Ottawa, Rosenberg decided to go there. By the time he arrived, he was penniless and destitute.

The former Czech ambassador eventually lost his position under the new Communist regime and, to earn a living, set up a small coffee shop with his wife on Rideau Street in the market district. Rosenberg was hired to do the dishes. After that he worked for a business for which he was never paid. Eventually Sam Berger, a prominent lawyer, took him in, though Rosenberg could not practise law without the required Canadian legal education.

From his applications to various government departments for positions, as well as correspondence with others in the Ottawa community, it is clear Rosenberg felt he rightfully deserved a break in Ottawa based on his position and education. It didn't take him long to realize that wasn't going to happen. Being one to persevere, Rosenberg went on to become a prominent businessman, a successful academic and a respected painter, as well as a notable philanthropist in the Ottawa community. He worked extensively on various committees established to help refugees make their way to Canada and call it home. He eventually established the International House on Somerset Street in Ottawa for students arriving in Canada from foreign countries. He spoke little of his experiences during and after the Second World War. It was only just before his death in 1986, that Rosenberg finally decided to begin telling the story of his involvement in the flight of the Theresienstadt orphans, as well as his other activities in the Second World War period. He never got a chance to finish the task.

Imre Yitzhak Rosenberg was a quiet, unassuming man, with a vision that often exceeded those of others around him. He was defiantly Jewish in a way that achieved positive results for thousands of other Jews during his time. Yet his story has never been completely or accurately conveyed, either as part of the existing public record or as a new addition to the millions of other historical accounts of the Holocaust.

We have come to doubt historical records. This is because so many events often prove to be different than they are commonly perceived, so many half-truths and untruths have been told, so many other truths embellished and so many stories made up glorifying individuals or events that truthfully don't deserve to be glorified. To be sure, many questions do arise relating to Rosenberg's story. Why did he wait forty years to make his involvement known? What did he hope to gain personally by altering the perception of those who knew of the events leading up to the flight of the orphans of Theresienstadt but never knew of Rosenberg's involvement?

Rosenberg's main intention in the last years of his life was to set the record straight. For too long he had kept quiet, even when historical records printed incorrect information and when universities around the world took that information as fact and taught it to their students. Since 1971, the *Holocaust Encyclopedia*, published by Yad Vashem in Jerusalem, has claimed that fewer than 100 children survived the Theresienstadt concentration camp, which is an error that has since been disproved.

"My husband was a wonderful man who had no desire to bolster his curriculum vitae by listing his own accomplishments," says Truda Rosenberg. "I don't think he really viewed them as medals, such as one would pin on a lapel. He always did what he thought was right and what he thought was best. At times, it seemed like he was almost thoughtless about his own needs, but that was the way he was. His story would never have been told at all had he not encountered such incredulous hostility when he tried to correct others whose accounts were missing information or were simply inaccurate.

"His final task before he died was to set the record straight, but he never had an opportunity to do so. The importance in this is not to establish who did what or wether this person did more than that person. One of the most important aspects of remembering the Shoah is to ensure that all people have the most complete and accurate record possible. That is what my husband wanted. And that is what all the others deserve."

The tales of many others who made liberation possible and who arranged for those Jews who remained in concentration camps after the Second World War to be moved back to their home towns, Israel or to North America, have also escaped pen and paper. Sometimes it's because their stories have simply been overlooked. In other cases, it's because historians didn't deem their stories worth telling to a general audience. In still others, heroic acts during and after the Second World War have never been documented for the simple reason that those individuals never thought it necessary to advertise their deeds.

ENDNOTES

[1] Theresienstadt is also referred to as Terezin throughout this piece. Terezin is the Czech name for the camp, while Theresienstadt is the German name.

[2] National Public Archives of Canada. Personal notes, 1932. Vol. 5, file 18.

[3] National Public Archives of Canada. Personal notes, 1932. Vol. 5, file 20.

[4] National Public Archives of Canada. Imre Rosenberg's work during the Second World War: photocopies of research material and correspondence. Vol. 5, file 24.

[5] Address given at the Second International Historical Conference at attempts at rescuing Jews during the Holocaust. April 8-11, 1974. Hlinka refers to Hlinka's Slovak Catholic Party, a political movement known to be supported by Germany; Jozef Tiso was its leader.

[6] Holocaust in Hebrew

[7] National Public Archives of Canada. Vol. 5, file 18. Letter to the editor of the Jerusalem Post, June 21, 1985.

[8] Sala Newton was also a Theresienstadt orphan and a member of the '45 Aid Society. She also had contact through correspondence with Rosenberg in 1985.

[9] National Public Archives of Canada. Vol. 5, file 21. Letter from Ben Helfgott, director of the 45 Aid Society, to Imre Rosenberg. Aug. 27, 1985.

[10] National Public Archives of Canada. Letters to Theresienstadt orphans for research purposes. 1985.

[11] Interview with Dr. Truda Rosenberg. October 1996. Ottawa.

[12] National Public Archives of Canada. Imre Rosenberg's work during the Second World War: photocopies of research material and correspondence. Vol. 5, file 26.

[13] Letter to A.J. Rosenberg in Tel Aviv, Israel from I. J. Rosenberg in Ottawa, Canada. July 21, 1952.

[14] Interview with Lipa Tepper, an 18-year-old Theresienstadt orphan. November 1996.

[15] Rosenberg's personal account of Theresienstadt upon his arrival on May 11, 1945. National Public Archives of Canada, vol. 5, file 31.

[16] Rosenberg's personal account of Theresienstadt upon his arrival on May

11, 1945. National Public Archives of Canada, vol. 5, file 31.

17 Interview with Samuel Hilton, formerly Schmuel Holckiener, a 15-year-old orphan of Theresienstadt. October 1996.

18 Interview with Litzi Sonnenschein, a five-year-old orphan of Theresien-stadt. December 1996.

19 National Public Archives of Canada. Imre Rosenberg's work during the Second World War: research material. Vol. 5, file 27.

20 National Public Archives of Canada. Imre Rosenberg's work during the Second World War: research material and correspondence. Vol. 5, file 30.

21 From the Zionist Review, London. August 24, 1945.

22 Telegram sent to Foreign Office from Home Office on Rosenberg's behalf requesting arrangements be made for the transfer of the orphans. May 28, 1945. From the National Public Archives of Canada. Vol. 5, file 29.

23 Telegram from Mrs. Nathan to Miss Fellner, Central Refugees Committee. June 2, 1945, copied to Mr. Prestige, Home Office. From the Central Zionist Archives, Jerusalem.

24 Telegram from Mrs. Nathan to Mr. Prestige at British Home Office, July 1, 1945.

25 Telegram sent to the Home Office from the Central Office for Refugees, or Foreign Office in Prague, on behalf of Dr. I. Rosenberg, May 18, 1945. From the Central Zionist Archives, Jerusalem.

26 Letter sent from Foreign Office in Prague to Home Office in London confirming acceptance of Theresienstadt orphans and acknowledging Rosenberg's involvement in arranging for transport. June 28, 1945.

27 Copy of telegram from Foreign Office to Prague confirming flight of Theresienstadt orphans to England. July 6, 1945.

28 Rosenberg's personal memoirs. From the National Archives of Canada, vol. 5, file 30.

29 Rosenberg's personal memoirs. From the National Archives of Canada, vol. 5, file 28.

30 Brown, M. Don, J.F. Evacuation to Westmoreland: From Home & Europe, 1939-1945. Doctorate thesis.(1946.

31 Telegram from Foreign Office to Prague, following from Fellner and Nathan, to I. J. Rosenberg in Prague. August 9, 1945.

32 Interview with Litzi Sonnenschein, orphan survivor of Theresienstadt.

December 1996.

[33] Interview with Samuel Hilton, a 15-year-old orphan survivor of Theresienstadt. October 1996.

[34] National Public Archives of Canada. Letter to Sophie Caplan regarding research into the orphans of Theresienstadt. Vol. 5, file 31.

[35] Brown, M. Don, J.F. Evacuation to Westmoreland: From Home & Europe, 1939-1945. Ph.D. D. thesis.(1946.

[36] The Jewish Chronicle, August 24, 1945. P.1.

[37] Interview with Dr. Truda Rosenberg. October 1996.

[38] Interview with Dr. Truda Rosenberg. October 1996.

BIBLIOGRAPHY

BOOKS

Abells, Chana. *Children we Remember*. Greenwillow, New York. 1986.

Allen, William S. *The Nazi Seizure of Power: The Experience of a Single German Town, 1922-1945*. Franklin Watts, New York. 1984.

Bauer, Yehudah. *Flight & Rescue: Brichah*. Random House, New York. 1970.

Bachrach, Susan. *Tell Them What We Remember: The Story of the Holocaust*. Little, Brown and Company, Boston. 1994.

Braham, R.L. *The Politics of Genocide: The Holocaust in Hungary*. New York. 1981.

Bridgman, Jon. *The End of the Holocaust: The Liberation of the Camps*. Areopagitica Press, Portland, Oregon. 1990.

Chaikin, Miriam. *A Nightmare in History: The Holocaust 1933-1945*. Houghton Mifflin, Boston. 1987.

Dagan, Avigdor. *The Jews of Czechoslovakia. Vols. I-III.* The Hebrew Publication Society of America, Philadelphia. 1984.

Dawidowicz, Lucy. *A Holocaust Reader*. Behrman House Publishers, New York. 1976.

Dawidowicz, Lucy. *The War Against the Jews* 1933-1945. Bantam, New York. 1986.

Dwork, Deborah. *Children with a Star: Jewish Youth in Nazi Europe*. Yale University Press, New Haven, CT. 1991.

Epstein, Helen. *Children of the Holocaust*. Viking Penguin, New York. 1988.

Gilbert, Martin. *The Holocaust: A History of the Jews in Europe during the Second World War.* Henry Holt & Co., New York. 1986.

Gilbert, Martin. *'The Boys'*. Simon & Schuster, London. 1996.

Grobman A, Landes, D. *Genocide: Critical Issues of the Holocaust*. Simon Wiesenthal Center, Los Angeles. 1983.

Grobman, A. *Genocide and Critical Issues of the Holocaust*. Simon Wiesenthal Center, Los Angeles. 1983.

Hillberg, Raul. *The Destruction of the European Jews.* (Three volumes.) Holmes and Meier, New York. 1985.

Hillberg, Raul. *Perpetrators, Victims, Bystanders: The Jewish Catastrophe, 1933-1945.* HarperCollins, New York. 1992.

Kavka, Frantisek. *An Outline of Czechoslovak History*. Orbis, Prague. 1963.

Kerner, R.J. ed. *Czechoslovakia*. University of California Press, Los Angeles. 1949.

Kushner, Tony. *The Holocaust and the Liberal Imagination. A Social and Cultural History*. Blackwell, Oxford, U.K. 1994.

Kushner, Tony. *The Persistence of Prejudice. Anti-Semitism in British Society during the Second World War*. Manchester University Press, England. 1989.

Levin, Nora: *The Holocaust: The Nazi Destruction of European Jewry, 1933-1945*. Kieger Publishing Co., Melbourne, Fl.. 1990.

Marrus, Michael. *The Holocaust in History*. New American Library / Dutton, New York. 1989.

Rogasky, Barbara: *Smoke and Ashes: The Story of the Holocaust*. Holiday House, New York. 1988.

Sachar, Abram. *The Redemption of the Unwanted. From the Liberation of the Death Camps to the Founding of Israel*. St. Martin's, New York. 1983.

Wasserstein, Bernard. *Vanishing Diaspora: The Jews of Europe since 1945*. Brandeis University Press, Boston. 1996.

ACADEMIC ARTICLES

Don, J.F. and Brown, *M.A. Evacuation to Westmoreland. From Home to Europe, 1939-1945*. (c) 1946.

Fierzova, Olga. *The Fates of the Children of the Post-War Time*. in Yivo Annual 23, No. 127. June 1985.

Moskovitz, Sarah. *Love Despite Hate. Child Survivors of the Holocaust and Their Adult Lives*. Schocken Books, New York. 1985.

Robinson, Jacob and Sachs, Henry. *The Holocaust: The Nuremberg Evidence, Part 1*. Yad Vashem, Jerusalem. 1976.

Rothkirchen, Livia. *The Czechoslovak Government-in-Exile: Jewish and Palestinian Aspects in the Light of Documents*. Yad Vashem Studies 9 (1973): 157-199.

PUBLISHED COLLECTIONS

Canadian Jewish Congress National Archives

CJC plenary resolution for Precious Legacy Exhibit. Central Zionist Archives, Jerusalem.

Jewish Agency for Palestine papers

World Jewish Congress papers

Greater London Record Office.
  Board of Deputies of British Jews archives Air Historical Branch:
    British Ministry of Defense.
  Official flight records of RAF activities.

PRIVATE COLLECTIONS
  National Public Archives of Canada
  Imre Yitzhak Rosenberg papers. MG 31, H 158. Finding Aid No.
    1383. (c) 1987.

GENERAL ARCHIVES:
  American Society for Yad Vashem, New York
  Terezin Ghetto Museum, Terezin, Czechoslovakia.
  Zidovske Museum Praha — Jewish Museum, Prague.
  State Central Archives, Prague.

NEWSPAPERS AND JOURNALS
  England: *Times of London, Daily Telegraph, The Guardian, Sunday Times*
  Canada: *Ottawa Citizen, Toronto Star, Globe and Mail, Montreal Gazette*
  U.S.:   *Boston Globe, New York Times, Washington Post*
  Jewish: *Jewish Quarterly, Jewish Chronicle, Jewish Standard, Zionist Review,*
            Canadian Jewish News, Ottawa Jewish Bulletin

INDIVIDUAL INTERVIEWS
Dr. Truda Rosenberg, Imre Rosenberg's wife. Ottawa, Canada.
Dr. Erica Barber, Theresienstadt survivor. Montreal, Canada.
Gerhart M. Riegner, World Jewish Congress, Geneva.
Dr. Elizabeth Eppler, Zionist Archives, Jerusalem.
Sophie Caplan, Theresienstadt orphan, Sydney, Australia.
Joanna Millan, Theresienstadt orphan, London.
Samuel Hilton, Theresienstadt orphan, Scottsdale, Arizona.
Wolf Rosenblatt, Theresienstadt orphan, Toronto.
Henry Lemberg, Theresienstadt orphan, Sydney, Australia. Litzi Sonnenschein,
  Theresienstadt orphan, Melbourne, Australia.
Ben Helfgott, Director of the '45 Aid Society and a Theresienstadt orphan,
  London, England.

Dr. Imrich Yitzhak Rosenberg
27 May 1913 – 26 June 1986

"With sadness, I read the obituary on the passing of Dr. Imrich Yitzhak Rosenberg of Ottawa. It must have brought a tear to many an eye of the people whose path ever crossed with Dr. Rosenberg. The life story of this remarkable man is how a community leader rose up to challenge the darkest days of the Munich betrayal, the collapse and occupation of Czechoslovakia, and the horrors of the approaching war. His unlimited service to the Jewish community, his devotion to saving Jewish lives, his efforts during the war and on the ashes of his liberated homeland, stand as a living memorial for all of us ... to learn, to admire and to cherish. To the list of his accomplishments may I also add that he was instrumental in the transfer to England of 301 children, orphans, from the Terezin camp during the Second World War. Some of these children of Terezin live in Canada and share this loss with the 'family'."

— Letter to the *Canadian Jewish News*

25TH
ANNIVERSARY
EDITION

PENUMBRA
PRESS